Container Gardening
Indoors and Out

Container

Gardening Indoors and Out

Jack Kramer

Doubleday & Company, Inc.
Garden City, New York

Library of Congress Catalog Card Number 78–103763
Copyright © 1971 by Jack Kramer
All Rights Reserved
Printed in the United States of America
9   8   7   6   5   4   3   2

Preface: Container Gardening,
Yesterday and Today

Container gardening is not new. The Hanging Gardens of Babylon, the Adonis Gardens of Greece, Domitian's Palace in Rome were decorated with plants in pots. But perhaps pot gardening really got its start in Spain when the Moors ruled. Here, gardens were open living spaces. In Versailles, the fabulous gardens abounded with tubbed orange trees and fancy urns brimming with flowers, and this gardening practice spread through Europe. And during the Renaissance in Italy, pot plants were a common feature of the garden, as they are today. Chinese gardens, too, were beautifully accented with container plants.

Today, in Greece, Spain, Italy, South America, and Mexico—wherever climates are temperate all year—open courtyards and gardens are part of the scene. And these areas are filled with potted plants. So are balconies and window sills.

In our country, too, patios and terraces are part of the American way of life even in climates where summers are short. The garden landscape has become part of the house, and these areas demand living plants in containers to make them attractive.

Now, gardening reaps vast rewards. Indoors, you can have colorful plants—not just old-fashioned favorites but new trees and shrubs—to decorate rooms. Outdoors, colorful new containers make gardening exciting. Trees and shrubs in decorative tubs are stellar displays, and growing them successfully requires different considerations than growing plants in the ground or in pots at windows. Now, the right plant in the right pot is a thing of beauty indoors or out. It is immediate accent, instant color where you want it and when you want it. Is it any wonder that container gardening is popular?

I am often asked by gardeners to clarify the container situation. There are so many pots and tubs and so many plants to put into them. Virtually, any kind of plant can be grown in some container, either permanently or temporarily. While I cannot do justice to all the plants that are commonly grown in containers, I have included in this book the ones that have an outstanding feature or that are more dependable than others.

This book is a guide to growing plants in containers on patio, terrace, in a garden room or sun porch, in living room or dining room—any room in the home.

JACK KRAMER

Mill Valley, California

Contents

Contents

Illustrations

Illustrations

 *Acknowledgments*

I offer thanks to the manufacturers of plant containers who willingly furnished photos and information about their products for my book. These include the Architectural Pottery Company of Los Angeles, California, Placet Products of Minneapolis, Minnesota, and the McGuire Furniture Company of San Francisco, California.

Special gratitude to the California Redwood Association for allowing me to have access to their photo file and to Pan American Seed Company for their photo help. To photographers Molly Adams, Jack Roche, and Joyce R. Wilson, a big thank-you for your cooperation and quick service in answering my photo requests.

To Simon and Schuster, for permission to use, in slightly different form in the section, "Battle Gardens and Terrariums," material from *Gardens under Glass*.

To Bob Behme and Roy Elliot, sincere appreciation for allowing me to use their photographs illustrating bonsai pots and sink gardens.

And finally, special thanks to Lolita Werner, who read, re-read, and did final checking of copy for this book.

JACK KRAMER

Part One
The Containers

1. On this wooden deck, plants in Spanish pots are featured to make a charming entrance. (*Molly Adams*)

2. In this garden room, a wooden basket is the container for a bright fuchsia. (*Joyce R. Wilson*)   3. A simple bowl is the container for this dish garden of succulents. (*Joyce R. Wilson*)   4. Novelty containers with succulents are cheerful additions to this area. (*Joyce R. Wilson*)   5. A redwood tub with an attractively shaped small tree is a feature of this room corner. (*California Redwood Assn.*)

3

4

5

6. This corner is decorated with a hanging basket and a large dracaena marginata in a square container. *(Placet Products)*

 *1. Containers Galore*

Today there are a bewildering number of containers for gardening. Choice becomes vital. Some plants are airy in appearance and need a bright, bold pot to show them off; others are bushy plants that need simple containers. A patio should be pleasing in all aspects—plants, pots, setting—and containers become part of the furnishings. What looks good in one pot will not necessarily be handsome in another. The right plant in the right pot placed in the proper area gives the unity and balance needed to make an outdoor living area or an indoor room beautiful.

Pots and Tubs

The standard clay pot was one of the earliest containers to be used. Today it comes in sizes from 3 to 24 inches in diameter. Soil in it dries out quickly, so there is little chance of overwatering plants. The clay pot is easy to use, inexpensive, and the natural clay color harmonizes with indoor and outdoor settings. Recently, many variations of the standard pot have appeared.

3

The Italian pot modifies the border to a tight-lipped detail; it is simple and good-looking. Some have round edges, others are beveled or rimless in sizes from 12 to 24 inches.

Venetian pots are barrel-shaped with a concentric band design pressed into the sides. Somewhat formal in appearance, they come in 8- to 20-inch sizes.

Spanish pots are graceful and always charming, with outward sloping sides and flared lips in 8- to 12-inch sizes. They have heavier walls than conventional pots and make good general containers for many plants.

Bulb pans or seed bowls are generally less than half as high as wide. They look like deep saucers but have drain holes in them. They are available in 6- to 12-inch sizes.

The azalea pot or fern pot, a squatty clay container formerly sold in only a few sizes is now offered from 6 to 14 inches in diameter. It is three quarters as high as it is wide and is in better proportion to most plants than conventional pots.

Three-legged pots are new, and bring the bowl shape to the indoor or outdoor garden. By raising the plant off a surface, these containers put it somewhat more on display. They range in size from 8 to 20 inches.

The cylindrical terra-cotta pot is a recent innovation. It is indeed handsome and a departure from the traditional tapered design. At present, it is available in three sizes with a maximum 14-inch diameter.

Terra-cotta strawberry jars and pots shaped like donkeys or chickens with planting holes are at nurseries too.

All new unglazed pots should be soaked overnight before they are used, otherwise, they absorb the water from the soil needed by the plants.

Architectural Pottery Company of Los Angeles, California, manufactures a handsome array of containers. These are high-fired clay planters in a wide range of related shapes and forms (too many to list here) keyed to today's architecture. They come in an unglazed off-white finish or glazed in colors, with or without drainage holes, and they are available through architects and interior designers.

1. A collection of handsome pots and tubs in varying sizes for small, medium, or large plants. (*Architectural Pottery Co.*)

Although the unglazed pot is most popular, glazed containers in many colors are attractive too. However, most of them are without drainage holes, so watering plants in them must be done moderately. It is difficult to know when the bottom of the pot is filled with waterlogged soil that will kill plants. If you use these decorative pots, take them to a glass store and have drain holes drilled. Or merely slip a potted plant into one of them.

Plastic pots are lightweight and come in many colors in round or square shapes. They are easy to clean and hold water longer than clay pots, so plants in them require less frequent watering—an advantage to some gardeners. They are not suitable for large plants as they have a tendency to tip over.

Tubs may be round, square, or hexagonal. If wooden, be sure they are made of durable wood such as redwood or cypress to resist decay. Stone or concrete tubs are ornamental, add dimension to a patio, and they are perfect for perennials.

5

2. Duraclay outdoor pots that take severe weather are ideal for small trees and shrubs; available in colors. (*Architectural Pottery Co.*) 3. A wood container and platform base are appealing either indoors or out. (*McGuire Furniture Co.*)

Tapered bowls are especially pretty filled with petunias and marigolds.

Japanese soy tubs are inexpensive, handsome on the patio, and plants look good in them. They are found at nurseries and basket shops. Wood and bamboo tubs with large foliage plants are also effective outdoors, as are galvanized washtubs painted dark colors. Assorted tubs are shown in Chapter Three.

Sawed-off wine casks banded with galvanized iron are unique and make fine containers (two sizes: 20 inch and 26 inch). Barrels and kegs are different and come in many sizes. There are small ones to 12 inches and large ones to 24 inches; most are very decorative and plants grow well in them.

Flat-bottomed cylindrical jars for chemicals are occasionally seen as decorative containers. However, they do not have drainage holes; if you use them, be sure to put in a layer (about 2 inches) of small stones at the bottom before you add soil. Then water will not accumulate in the soil to turn it sour. Jars come in 13- to 24-inch diameters. Remember, these containers are, like all glass, breakable. Do handle with care.

6

Urns and Jardinieres

. Concrete, stone, or Fiberglas urns come in many different sizes. They are at their best when viewed at eye level, as on the end of a terrace wall. Petunias and geraniums are lovely in them. Pedestal urns are handsome, too, but usually large. They can overpower a small area, so use them with discretion. Stone baskets are happy choices for trailing plants like campanula and lobelia.

Glazed Japanese pots are stunning. If you have a special place that needs rich color, try one. The blue-glazed tubs are attractive with an irregular-shaped tree such as a black pine

4. This camellia is attractive in a simple tapered redwood box. Note the low platform under the container to protect the floor. (*Joyce R. Wilson*)

or a mugo pine. Other containers are Japanese porcelain urns, beautiful but not cheap.

Chinese ceramic pots in various round shapes are handsome and ideal for foliage plants like caladiums and dieffenbachias. They are generally glazed in blue or green hues. Some are extremely ornate, others simple. Perhaps not Chinese, but with Far East flavor, are brass pots and gold-leaf tubs. They make almost any common plant appear special.

Bonsai Pots (see Chapter 6).

Cachepots

The cachepot was originally designed as a colorful cover-up for flowerpots, but plants can also be put directly into them. These decorative containers come in many shapes, sizes, and materials. The porcelain ones, generally splashed with fruit and flower designs, are especially pleasing. The metal cachepot is handsome, too, and the many fine wooden ones of mahogany and teak are lovely but expensive.

I have also seen hexagonal cachepots with footed bases that add a note of elegance to any room, and the ones delicately etched with Greek border designs always bring comment from guests.

The choice of plants for these pots is varied, from ivy to bromeliads. It is a matter of your own personal tastes, but, generally, small plants are more desirable than large ones, which would be out of scale to the container. You can buy cachepots at any good gift shop.

Boxes

Trees and shrubs demand wooden boxes. The largest tub simply does not hold enough soil or carry enough visual weight to balance a tree. Some boxes are a perfect cube, others a low cube. In most cases, the simple box is fine. However, it can be somewhat more than a box with a little handiwork. Once you have the basic container there is much that can be

5. A simple white bowl can be used anywhere in the home or on the patio; use appropriate small plants for it. (*Architectural Pottery Co.*)

done to vary its design. There are a number of variations for boxes; let your imagination ramble. Dress them up (see Chapter 2).

A large box with a potted tree weighs several hundred pounds. If you are not in year-round temperate climate you will have to store the tree in winter. Buy the commercial dollies with wheels and put them under the boxes so they can be moved about easily. Or make your own moving devices with 2-inch casters and boards.

Planters and Window-boxes

Some homes are designed with built-in planters; they are wooden, with galvanized insert pans. Generally they are below windows, or in entry halls, or used as room dividers. Many homes are without these custom-made units, but there is always a living-room corner or dining alcove that is greatly enhanced by a planter at a window.

Planters for outdoors can be freestanding or of a stationary type of any given design—triangular, oblong, or rectangular. Used for patio borders or in corners, they are instant gardening. With geraniums and agapanthus the patio becomes colorful in one afternoon. Portable units can be rearranged at any time. Put them where you think they will look the best. They can be window-box size or be made to fit an area.

Stationary planters of brick, stone, or slate take time to make, but once built they are attractive. A trench must be dug about 20 inches in depth, depending on the local frost line of the area. These planters are handsome against a house wall (see Chapter 2).

In Europe, window-boxes are part of the architecture, and in this country they are gaining popularity. The window-box is merely another form of container, its shape and size designed for window use. There is something friendly and charming about these portable boxes; certainly, they decorate the outside of the house in a unique way. To use them to best advantage and to minimize maintenance, a little bit of thought about size and type of box saves a great deal of trouble later.

All kinds of materials are being used for boxes—concrete, metal, plastic—but to me, the old-fashioned wooden box is still the best. Redwood resists decay and weathers well—it turns a lovely silver color—and after trying other woods, it certainly is my choice. The outside of the box can be the natural finish or it can be painted a contrasting color to the house.

The size of the window dictates the size of the box. However, beware of very long window-boxes; they become too heavy filled with soil, and hanging them properly can be a problem. Two small ones would be better than one very large one. The most satisfactory dimensions are 10 inches wide, 12 inches deep, and 28 to 36 inches long (see Chapter 2).

Window-boxes are heavy and must be securely fastened to the building wall. Bolt them to wall studs or fasten them with lag screws. In addition, I install sturdy L-shaped iron brackets to support them. A 5-foot box filled with soil weighs about 400 pounds, a formidable hazard when dropped from a second-floor window.

If your outdoor season is short, it is best not to plant directly into the box. Merely set potted plants inside it. Fill

6. A permanent stone planter filled with lush flowering plants is a handsome feature in this garden. (*Belgian Begonia Association*)

in and around the pots with peat moss or sphagnum. There are advantages to this method. It is easy to move plants into the house when cool weather starts and it is not necessary to buy additional soil. Where winters are severe, window-boxes should be protected, otherwise they may crack. After removing the soil from them, cover the boxes with tarpaulin or plastic cloth, or try potted evergreens to fill them in winter.

The idea of window-box gardening is a sound one. Plants are exposed to the circulation of air on all sides, benefit from rain, and they have ample soil to grow in. Soil dries out rapidly in flower boxes, so frequent watering is necessary, sometimes twice a day in July and August. Use a general greenhouse soil for the boxes, and a month after planting start a regular feeding program as you do for house plants. Almost any kind of a plant can be grown in a window-box.

FOR FULL SUN

Geranium
Lantana
Lobelia
Nasturtium
Petunia

FOR PARTIAL SUN

Browallia
Semperfloren *begonia*
Impatiens
Heliotrope

FOR PARTIAL SHADE

Aeschynanthus
Episcia
Fuchsia
Tuberous *begonia*
Achimenes

12

VINES AND TRAILERS

Cobaea scandens
Thunbergia alata
Tuberous *begonias* (pendula type)
Bouganvillea

Vertical Gardens

Vertical gardens in boxes or flats are seldom seen, and yet they offer great charm and plants grow well in vertical positions. Drainage is excellent, plants are readily visible against a wall, and this is a unique feature for any garden. The mechanics of box gardens are simple; use a wire mesh (2½ inches) on a frame of wood. The box is lined with thin sheets of sphagnum moss and filled with soil. It may be built directly against a building wall or it can stand free, with access from both sides. The box that is to be planted on one side must be 6 to 8 inches thick with slat backing. A freestanding planter can be 8 to 12 inches thick.

Planting the box takes some preparation, but the extra time is well worth the beauty these gardens bring to a wall.

Fill the box with soil. Now, use plants with small root balls and push them into potting holes through the mesh of the wire. Plant deep and affix the plants slightly upwards. When the box is finished it can be fastened to a wall or a railing with hooks, or nailed in place if it is to be a permanent decoration.

Watering the plants in the box depends on the weather, the thickness of the container, and the plants grown. The idea is to keep the soil evenly moist through the warm months and somewhat drier the rest of the year.

There are many plants for vertical gardens. Begonias, impatiens, dwarf fuchsias, cacti, and succulents do especially well. But experiment and try other plants too. This is an adventure in gardening, and half the fun is in creating something different.

Architectural Fiberglas Containers

These planters enable the gardener to have containers that otherwise would be too large to make in clay. The material used is a Fiberglas-reinforced resin with integral colors and a selection of smooth or textured finishes. The material has exceptional strength, is maintenance free, and, because it is lightweight, the containers are ideal for roof decks, balconies, and other areas where weight may be a problem.

There is a wide variety of sizes and shapes: cylinders from 24 to 60 inches in diameter, convex squares, tapered shapes, and sculptural forms. They are made by the Architectural Pottery Company of Los Angeles, California.

The same company manufactures a Duraclay pot—a fusion of clay and reinforced plastic. The advantage of a Duraclay pot is that it is guaranteed unbreakable and freezeproof, so it can be left outdoors even in severe winters. It comes in many sizes and shapes and in several handsome finishes. The color range is incredible—from bright blue to brilliant orange. The exposed aggregate finish is in earth tones made up of multicolored granules, and blends beautifully with outdoor settings. The textured finish is grainy, suggesting masonry, and the smooth finish is subtle and pleasing.

There is a choice of pedestal pots, bowls, cylinders, and even shallow designs for bulbs and low-growing plants.

For indoor use, the pots come without drain holes unless you specifically ask that they be drilled. Rather than risk a waterlogged soil for plants, order containers that will drain. If it is absolutely necessary for pots to be watertight, use a cork mat under the container to protect surfaces from moisture.

Hanging Baskets

Hanging baskets suspended from eaves or rafters put plants in an enviable position to enjoy light. And indoors for sunny windows there are bracket holders for basket growing. But

7. A lush fern at eye level is a striking basket plant.
(*Hort-Pix*)

don't hang pots too high; you want to be able to water them.
Always provide some kind of receptacle for excess water drainage. The clip-on saucer that is available for baskets works well
for my plants. A stepladder or a step stool is almost essential
when you water basket plants, or at least a long beaked watering can. It saves walking back and forth to a sink to water
plants.

Today all kinds of hanging baskets are to be found at nurseries and florist centers. There are wooden ones, wire ones,
plastic kinds, and clay types. There are also one-of-a-kind containers from ceramists. Recently, bubble bowls suspended in
net or burlap have made their appearance and these make fine
accent baskets.

The open-slatted redwood basket commonly used for orchids

is a good one to work with. It looks something like an inverted tapered log cabin and allows sufficient circulation of air without rapid loss of moisture by evaporation through slatted sides. Conventional wire baskets are good, too. They are inexpensive, lightweight, and possibly the best of these containers. Line them with sphagnum moss or osmunda (tree fern fiber), and fill with mix.

Most baskets come with wire, chain, or rope for hanging. Simply put a screw eye or a clothesline hook into the ceiling or rafter edge and the plant is ready for hanging.

Where you place the basket depends largely on what you have to hang it from. The outer periphery of the patio is good— there are rafters or beams. At house windows, baskets are attractive and charming.

It is well to remember that plants hung too far above eye level are not easily seen, and they must not be in the way of room traffic. Being forced to duck around a plant is bothersome. So put hanging baskets in suitable places where they do not interfere with people and so that they are at proper eye level to give maximum effect. You want to enjoy the flowers and foliage to the fullest.

Novelty Containers

Novelty containers—kitchen pots, pails, jelly tubs, wheelbarrows, and donkey carts are other things in which to put a plant. There are also bird cages, animal figures with space for planting, and strawberry jars. Any of these used with discretion can make a room more attractive. Used with abandon, they clutter an area.

I recently found some woven bamboo pot covers that slip over the pots. These make containers attractive and are especially suitable for hiding soiled clay pots. The covers are simple and come in many sizes.

Natural Containers

Whether you select pieces of wood, natural rock, or seashore materials, using natural "containers" is fun. Plants appear different in them; texture and color of foliage complemented by organic materials are shown to their best advantage.

Rocks should be chosen with eroded pockets; the depressions do not have to be too deep. Size and shape are important. Not every one you find will be suitable for planting.

Select pieces of trees that are small and have decayed pockets in them to receive plants. Brush and clean wood and rocks with soap and water. Use a wire brush to bring textures to the surface.

If you cannot go to nature to find your containers they can be found in various shops. Pet stores that specialize in tropical fish usually have unique pieces of rock. Lavarock, a handsome volcanic-looking stone, is found at building suppliers. So is Featherrock. Planting pockets can be chipped into the materials. Driftwood can be found at novelty stores.

A bag of osmunda available at garden centers and some thin-gauge galvanized wire are necessary for planting. And you will need some light porous soil; I add sand to my regular greenhouse mix. The osmunda can be cut into chunks (after overnight soaking) and used as layers or liners. It gives the plant the necessary footing if the depression in the natural container is shallow. Pad the area with the osmunda and then fill with soil.

In some cases you will have to wire plants to natural "containers" until they really take hold. Place the plant firmly against the wood or stone in the desired position; push as much of the root system as you can into the soil or osmunda. Then wire the plants firmly to the host. It takes six months to a year before they are permanent, and then the wires can be cut and discarded.

Self-watering Containers

These are new, and what a boon for the gardener who is away from home a few days a week! The containers are cylindrical or square, white or in colors. At present, they come in

8. The Plantender automatic watering system regulates soil moisture by a sensor that can be used in any type plant. (*Courtesy Plantamation, Inc.*)

three sizes with the maximum 12 inches. No doubt there will be more sizes in the future. The containers are generally made of plastic, and the base that holds the water is removable. The number of wicks that extend from the pot determines the flow of water according to the type of plant and length of your absence. The water rises through the wick to supply the soil with moisture. Some models have tubes instead of wicks.

The manufacturer of the Florabien water planter states: "Soil stays moist two to four weeks without rewatering (five to ten days outdoors) depending on humidity and temperature."

18

This planter has a separate water bin in the bottom with a refill tube and water-level rod.

The Floramatic waterer is a glass vial that, filled with water, is inserted in soil and automatically dispenses water to the plant. This device can be used in any kind of pot.

The Plantender is an attractive, double-walled container that holds your potted plant. A reservoir between the walls holds sufficient water to last most plants several weeks. The time between refills depends on the size and type of plant, and other variables such as sun, heat, and humidity. The reservoir is operated by a unique moisture sensor that controls water content in the soil.

2. Make Your Own Containers

The nice thing about container gardening is that you can build many of the boxes and tubs. Fitting a box to a required area is easy, and custom detailing always looks best. Hanging baskets take little time to make, are easily assembled, and are inexpensive. Planters and window-boxes are other containers that can be made at home to suit your own tastes. Even concrete tubs can be attempted in the workshop.

Wood

Wood is the best material, and is the most popular for tubs and boxes. It lasts a long time, is easy to work with, and the natural finish looks good on patios and terraces. Redwood and cedar resist rot, weather beautifully over the years, and need no outside finish. For decorative effect, they can be scored or grooved or sandblasted.

Douglas fir is more costly than redwood but it is stronger and excellent for very large boxes. It needs preservative coating; the outside of the box can be stained to give it a finished appearance. Pine can also be used, but it is soft and must of course also be treated with a preservative available at hardware stores. A galvanized metal liner can be used inside the box instead of the protective coating, but it is expensive and must be custom made.

While boxes are generally nailed together, if you use glue and screws, they will last longer. Use brass screws and good quality wood glue. One-inch lumber is fine for most small boxes, but for larger containers use 2-inch stock.

The container with flared or tapered sides is handsome and suitable for dish gardens, annuals, almost any small planting. An 18-inch top tapering to a 10-inch base is a good size for many arrangements. Use 1-inch redwood or cedar for the box; miter the corners. Add a platform made from 1-inch lumber to give the box a finished look. For larger plants, build a 24-inch tapered box (see Illustration 9).

A simple rectangular box, 3 inches deep made from 1-inch redwood is ideal for small succulents, flowering bulbs, and other low-growing plants. I use brass screws to fasten the sides, ¾-inch stock for the bottom and 1- by 1-inch platform legs at each corner. These are nailed in place. After the box is finished, drill ¼-inch drain holes in the bottom.

The cube box is functional, neat, and simple. For a 12-inch box, 1- by 12-inch redwood is best. To give it a finished appearance you can stain the wood a dark color and then nail 1- by 1-inch wooden strips spaced ½ inch apart around it. For a larger container for a small tree or shrub, use 2- by 4-inch lumber and follow directions in Illustration 10.

Crosshatched containers similar to open-slatted redwood baskets can be made in several ways. They can be a box within a box or follow the instructions for a conventional redwood basket in Illustration 11.

A container made from acoustical tile board (14 by 14 inches or 16 by 16 inches) is another idea. Here, the boards are used for the four sides and 2-inch stock is used for corner posts and the bottom. A ¾-inch molding provides the top cap. Corner posts must be grooved so the boards can slide into position. Glue them in place and then notch each corner of the base to accommodate the posts. A variation of the same kind of container would be two sides of plywood and two sides of redwood.

Concrete

To make concrete containers, you need wood framing for the size of the box desired. The concrete mix should be fairly stiff: 3 parts cement, 1 part sand, and 2 parts pebbles. Or use Sakrete commercial mix and just add water. Pour the mix into the forms, put a presoaked standard clay pot in position, and fill in with concrete to the top of the frame. After the concrete is firm, scrub it with a wire brush, and twenty-four hours later strip off the wooden forms and take out the pot. Run water over the surface and scrub it with a wire brush.

Other concrete containers can be made by using two cardboard cartons. One should be small enough to leave 1½ to 2 inches of space at the bottom and four sides when placed inside the other one. Pour 2 inches of concrete mix into the bottom of the first carton. Tamp down; then put the smaller carton inside. Pour and tamp mix between the two cartons to make the walls of the planter. Cardboard forms can be removed in a day. Let the concrete dry slowly for a few days. Then, using a chisel, shape the planter. Scrub it with a wire brush and wet it down several times before using it. All sizes and shapes can be made using one of the two methods described above. For further details see Illustration 12.

For variation, an exposed aggregate finish can be made by scrubbing the concrete surface with a wire brush after it has set overnight. Or apply integral color pigment to the concrete before it is poured. Another possibility is to add beach pebbles to the mix for a contrasting texture.

Metallic Sheet Containers

A copper or tin box might fit into your setting better than a wooden one. They appear costly but are actually inexpensive to make if you buy copper or tin sheeting at a hardware store and simply cover a box with the material (see Illustration 13 for instructions).

Cylinders

Clay pipe cylinders and flue tiles offer limitless possibilities for do-it-yourself containers. In various diameters they come in terra cotta or in concrete color and can be found at building-supply yards.

The diameter of the pipe will dictate the use. I find the 16¼- by 17¼-inch pipe ideal for outdoor planters. I simply sink the cylinder a few inches into the ground for a permanent container. A more finished planter can be made by using exterior plywood for the bottom (see Illustration 14 for details).

Window-boxes

Because there is considerable pressure against the sides of the box, it must be built with care. If you are making your own planter, use 1-inch lumber and brass screws. Nails have a tendency to pull out if the boards warp. Angle irons at the corners give extra strength, and the necessary drainage holes must be drilled in the bottom of the box. It is important that the box be watertight at the corners and seams. Dripping water will discolor house walls. The holes should be placed at the front of the bottom of the box so that excess water drains away from house walls.

Be sure boxes are put in place 1 or 2 inches from the walls, another precaution against water-stained walls. Formerly, I used a metal liner inside the box, but this was expensive and impeded drainage. I now plant directly into the box and this seems satisfactory. Commercial window-boxes are also available if you do not have time to make your own. There are a variety of sizes and styles, some simple, others plain (see Illustration 15 for a different type of window-box).

Permanent Planters

In California, many homes include permanent planters of brick, wood, or concrete in the garden. Often, they are built to fit a special place. They can be rectangular, or square, or triangular, or circular. Like tubs and pots their value is largely decorative.

Outdoor planters attached to entrances or the front of a house should be in proper scale and in proportion to the building. Because they cannot be moved, they should have galvanized metal liners and adequate facilities for drainage. Although redwood planters are attractive in the garden, brick or bluestone boxes are superior in appearance.

Raised planter beds of brick look good in a garden and have advantages. They make bending easier when you weed and plant. They provide growing areas of excellent drainage, and the retaining walls of raised planters keep out greedy roots of nearby trees and shrubs. Also, raising the beds makes the flowers and foliage appear more decorative, bringing them closer to eye level.

To build a planter, lay out a line you want to follow on the ground and dig a trench about 15 inches deep. Make it 5 inches wider than the wall you are planning. Fill the trench with concrete, using 1 part cement, 3 parts sand, and 5 parts gravel. When the footing is dry, install the brick on it, using mortar and checking each brick with a level to make sure it is evenly placed. When the wall has reached the height you want, trim it off with a cap of concrete. Raised planters of this type can be used against a fence, as entranceway highlights, or as retaining walls around the edge of patios or walks. Free-form designs can be built around posts or trees.

When you select plants, give some thought to scale. Don't put large trees and shrubs in small boxes or small ones in large containers. Flowering plants are especially handsome in built-in planters while philodendron, aralia, and schefflera species make a lush picture, if not as colorful. Put crotons, hibiscus, and flowering maple in individual decorative containers. Cannas and hostas with large leaves are appealing in standard terracotta pots, more so than in the ground. Almost any kind of plant can be grown in raised beds and usually grows better than in the ground.

Terrariums

In a glass container, a miniature garden is something more than just a gathering of plants. It becomes a private little world. While the container for a diminutive landscape can be a brandy snifter, bubble bowl, or a bottle, it more often is an aquarium, or—when filled with plants—a terrarium.

Rather than buying an aquarium it is simple to make your own glass tank. And certainly it is one way to have green plants where home conditions will not support plant life. The terrarium by its very nature supplies its own humidity and temperature, and waters itself. Condensation on the glass runs into the soil, furnishing moisture for the plants.

To make a simple terrarium, have a glass shop cut four panes of double-strength window glass to the desired size. For a 16- by 20-inch container you will need two 12- by 16-inch sides, two 12- by 20-inch sides, and one 16- by 20-inch bottom of ¼-inch patterned glass.

Set up the four sides of the terrarium and seal at the corners with waterproof glass epoxy. Wrap small pieces of masking or binding tape around the corners to hold the glass in place until the epoxy sets. Then remove the tape. Put the cube on the glass bottom and glue in place with epoxy. For a top for the terrarium, use another sheet of double-strength window glass.

For a unique terrarium try the compartmented glass garden in Illustration 16.

(This and the construction drawings (9–16) which follow were prepared by Adrian Martinez)

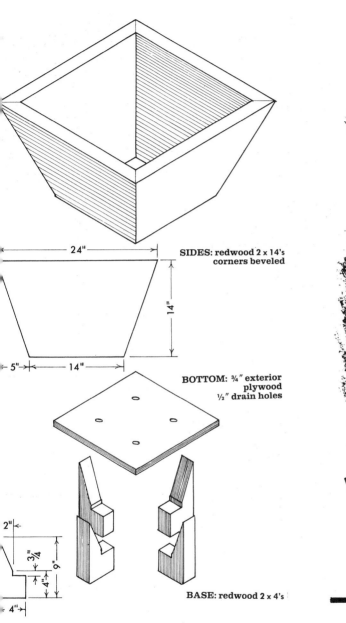

24"

SIDES: redwood 2 x 14's
corners beveled

14"

5" 14"

BOTTOM: ¾" exterior
plywood
½" drain holes

2"

3/4"

9"

4"

4"

BASE: redwood 2 x 4's

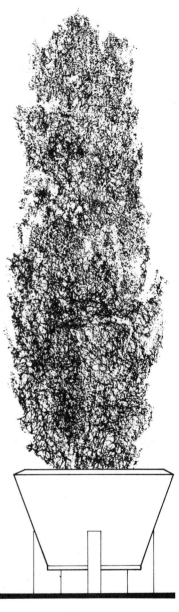

TAPERED BOX PLANTER

design / adrián martínez

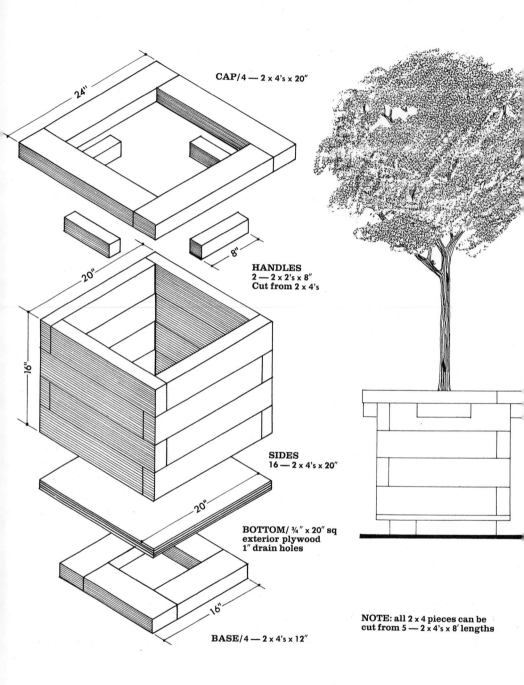

CAP/4 — 2 x 4's x 20"

24"

20"

8"

HANDLES
2 — 2 x 2's x 8"
Cut from 2 x 4's

16"

SIDES
16 — 2 x 4's x 20"

20"

BOTTOM/ ¾" x 20" sq
exterior plywood
1" drain holes

16"

BASE/4 — 2 x 4's x 12"

NOTE: all 2 x 4 pieces can be
cut from 5 — 2 x 4's x 8' lengths

TREE PLANTER BOX   design / adrián martínez

28

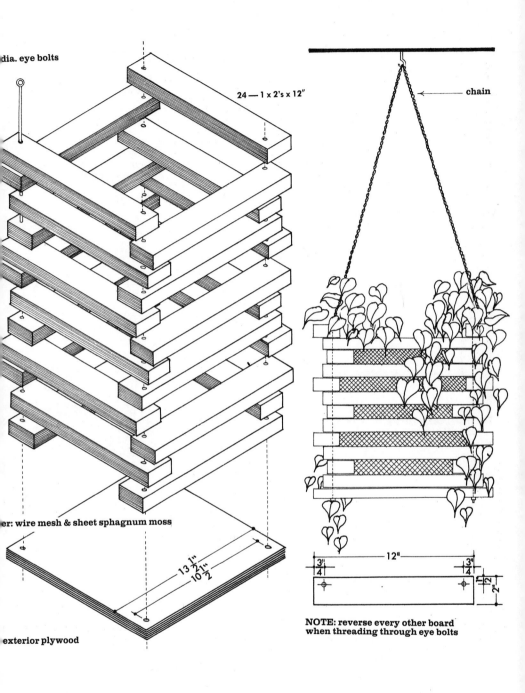

dia. eye bolts

24 — 1 x 2's x 12"

chain

er: wire mesh & sheet sphagnum moss

13 1"
2 1"
10 1"
2

exterior plywood

12"

3"
4

3"
4

2"

NOTE: reverse every other board
when threading through eye bolts

HANGING BASKET

design / adrián martínez

29

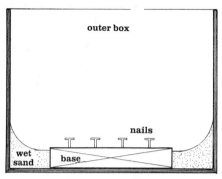

1. position base, mold sand to shape

MATERIALS:

1. HEAVY CARDBOARD BOXES
2. REDWOOD BLOCK (BASE)
3. HEAVY NAILS
4. SAND (MOLD & WEIGHT)
5. WIRE MESH (REINFORCING)
6. CONCRETE
   1 part cement
   1 part sand
   1 ½ parts vermiculite
   (or other lightweight aggregate)
   coloring powder
stir dry, add water to make a stiff mix

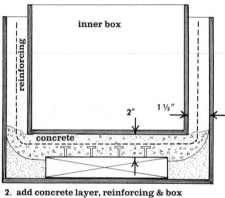

2. add concrete layer, reinforcing & box

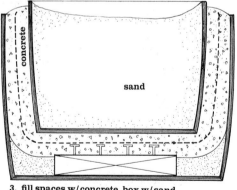

3. fill spaces w/concrete, box w/sand
   remove boxes after 12 to 24 hours

4. shape & smooth w/rasping tools & wire brush

CONCRETE PLANTER

design / adrián martínez

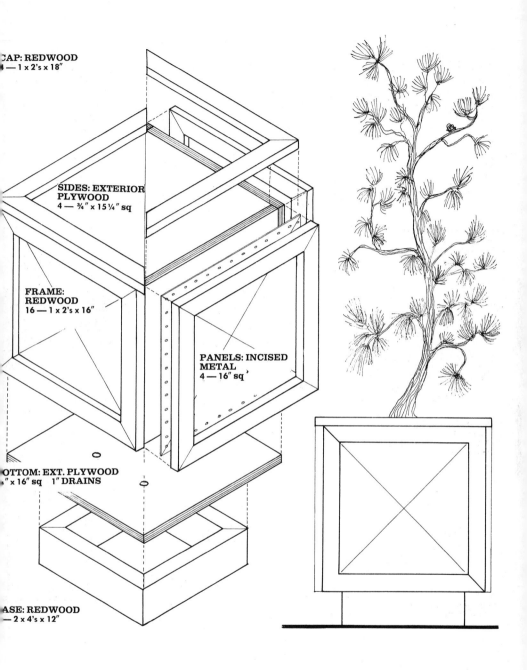

CAP: REDWOOD
4 — 1 x 2's x 18"

SIDES: EXTERIOR
PLYWOOD
4 — ¾" x 15¼" sq

FRAME:
REDWOOD
16 — 1 x 2's x 16"

PANELS: INCISED
METAL
4 — 16" sq

BOTTOM: EXT. PLYWOOD
" x 16" sq   1" DRAINS

BASE: REDWOOD
— 2 x 4's x 12"

SHEET METAL BOX   design / adrián martínez

31

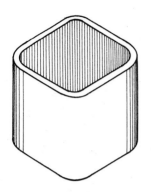

SIDES: tile flues—several sizes & shapes in earth colors are available

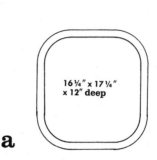

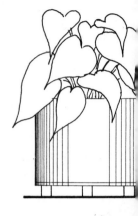

a

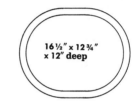

16 ¼″ x 17 ¼″ x 12″ deep

BOTTOM: ¾″ exterior plywood epoxied to flue (follow directions carefully) ½″ drain holes

b

16 ½″ x 12 ¾″ x 12″ deep

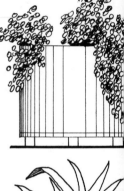

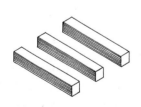

BASE: redwood 2 x 2's nailed to bottom

c

12 ½″ x 12 ½″ x 12″ deep

TILE FLUE PLANTERS

design / adrián martínez

32

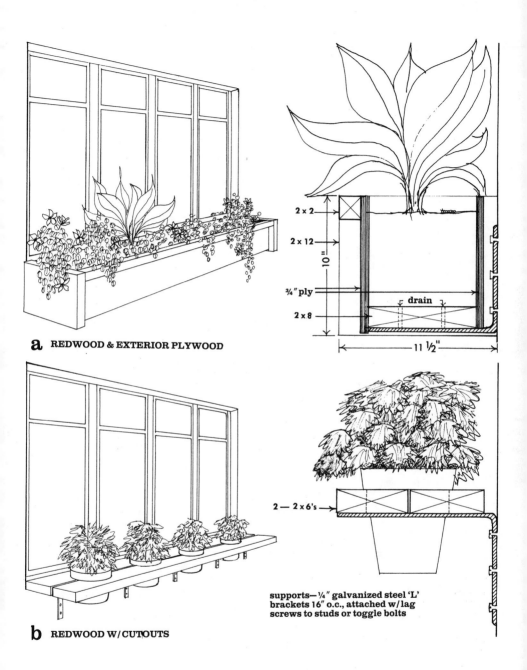

a REDWOOD & EXTERIOR PLYWOOD

2 x 2
2 x 12
10"
¾" ply   drain
2 x 8

|← 11 ½" →|

b REDWOOD W/CUTOUTS

2 — 2 x 6's

supports— ¼" galvanized steel 'L'
brackets 16" o.c., attached w/lag
screws to studs or toggle bolts

WINDOW BOXES

design / adrián martínez

33

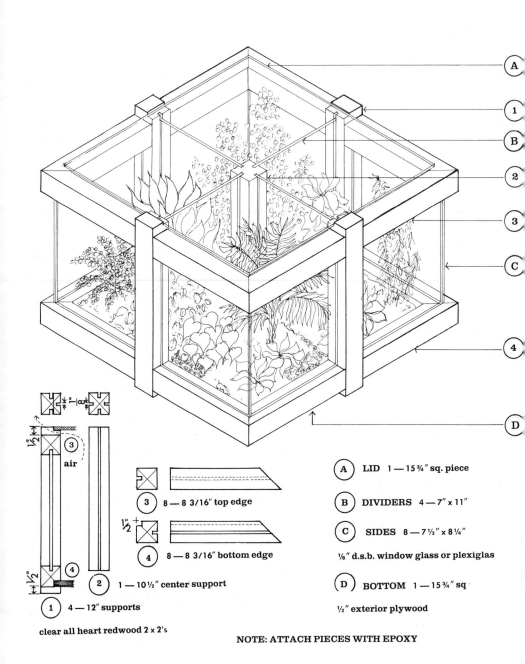

A   LID   1 — 15¾″ sq. piece

B   DIVIDERS   4 — 7″ x 11″

C   SIDES   8 — 7½″ x 8¼″

⅛″ d.s.b. window glass or plexiglas

D   BOTTOM   1 — 15¾″ sq

½″ exterior plywood

3   8 — 8 3/16″ top edge

4   8 — 8 3/16″ bottom edge

2   1 — 10½″ center support

1   4 — 12″ supports

clear all heart redwood 2 x 2's

NOTE: ATTACH PIECES WITH EPOXY

GLASS GARDEN

design / adrián martínez

34

 *3. Maintenance and Care*
of Containers and Plants

After plants are selected and put in tubs or boxes, container gardening is no more—and perhaps less—work than gardening in the ground. Plants are close by on the patio or in the garden, and it is easy to water them. They are elevated; they are easier to tend. And while flying insects may attack the plants, many of the crawling pests never reach them at all.

A good container should have ample provisions for draining excess water from it. At the same time, it must be made of materials to withstand watering and drying out. And it must be built to take stress and strain of the soil within it. To help prevent decaying in certain types of wood, put wooden cleats or blocks under the box to increase air circulation. Air space under containers also eliminates hiding places for insects.

Indoors, use trays or stain-resistant saucers—with protective coating—under containers. It is a good idea to elevate pots, too, with small wooden blocks under them in saucers.

Selecting a Container

The largest tub or box at nurseries is 28 inches. If you are growing a very large tree or shrub (over 6 feet) you will have to make a container for it. This is not difficult and can be done in less than an hour (see Chapter 2).

Choose a container that is in proportion and in character with the plant you want to grow. Generally, bushy specimens like podocarpus or pittosporum look best in tubs. Sculptural branching plants like pomegranate, loquat, and citrus are handsome in wooden boxes, and standards (plants grown to tree form) and large palms are especially suitable for Spanish pots. Lacy plants like bamboo and *ficus benjamina* are more in keeping with ornate containers—a jardiniere or an urn, perhaps.

Beware of brightly colored containers—they can steal the show from a plant. Pots of neutral colors—beige, off-white, terra cotta—or redwood tubs are better foils for leaf and flower. Remember to soak all unglazed containers—old or new—in water for about six hours before using them so they will not absorb the moisture needed by the plant. Take the time to scrub them with soap and water, not only to remove dirt but to eliminate insect eggs and fungus spores that may be present.

A 16-inch-square box 12 inches high weighs about 250 pounds, a devil to move. Provide wheels or dollies under heavy containers so you can move them around if necessary. Ready-made platforms with wheels are at nurseries or you can make your own with 2- by 4-inch boards and casters.

As mentioned, there are numerous containers. What you choose depends on the plant you are growing and your own individual tastes. Wooden boxes and planters are probably the first choice of most gardeners. They are lightweight, they do not heat up unduly in sun, and they come in many sizes. While many different kinds of wood can be used, redwood is easiest to work with and needs no protective coating. Cypress and Douglas fir (with preservatives) are satisfactory too. Terra-cotta pots are also popular. They are porous and water evaporates from them readily, they come in many sizes and shapes and blend well with plantings, but they are heavy to move and plants in them require frequent watering.

Plastic containers of Fiberglas are lightweight and come in many colors. They are easy to clean, almost unbreakable, and generally inexpensive. However, they hold moisture longer than clay or concrete pots, and with large plants in them, they have a tendency to tip over.

17. A selection of wooden containers for plants. Some are stained, some left natural. (*Modernage Photo*)

18. Gold-leaf tubs are elegant choices for plants and really put them on display. (*Joyce R. Wilson*)

Metal containers are handsome but they are rarely durable. The weight of the soil may buckle them, and in sun they gather excessive heat. Concrete and concrete-and-perlite containers can be used, too, but they are heavy and have a tendency to chip.

Potting Mixes

The kind of potting mix you use depends on your individual climate and the type of plant being grown. Choose soil that will hold moisture and yet allow drainage of excess water freely. Waterlogged soil quickly kills container plants.

There are a great many potting mixes for plants. Nurseries have soil in sacks, building-supply yards have it in bulk, and some florists will sell it in bushels. I use a basic garden mix of 1 part garden loam, 1 part sand, and 1 part leaf mold. I add more sand to the mix for cacti and succulents, and for acid-loving azaleas and camellias I substitute 1 part peat moss to the mix instead of the leaf mold. My orchids and bromeliads are in equal parts of shredded fir bark and garden soil.

Some growers use perlite mixed with soil, others prefer peat moss or sphagnum moss, and so on.

Growing media that contains no soil have earned much discussion in recent years. These mixes are referred to as peat-like mixes and evolved from several years of research at Cornell University. Basically, they are composed of sphagnum peat moss and horticultural perlite or vermiculite. Sufficient nutrients must be added to them for plant growth. While the mixes are lightweight—an advantage in container gardening—plants in them must be fed regularly. Be prepared to devote more time to plants in peat-like mixes.

For one peck combine:

4 quarts dry measure vermiculite
4 quarts dry measure shredded peat
1 level tablespoon ground limestone
1 level tablespoon 5-10-15 fertilizer

19. Simple soy tubs are fine for many plants; inexpensive. (*Joyce R. Wilson*)

Potting and Repotting

Whatever growing medium you use, it will have to be renewed in time. Generally, plants in large boxes (16 inches or over) can go several years without repotting; smaller containers need fresh soil more often. Repot a plant when roots grow out of the bottom of the container or when the root ball has compacted and you see roots on the surface of the soil. Exceptions are clivias and some succulents that like to be crowded (pot-bound) in a pot. With these, dig out the top 3 to 4 inches of soil and replace with fresh mix. Spring and fall are the best times to repot plants. In spring, warm weather helps plants adjust to new conditions, and in fall, there is still time for plants to grow before cold weather starts.

To remove a plant from a small or medium container (to 14 inches) rap the sides of the box or tub sharply with a hammer. If you can lift it, rap the container against a table edge. Grasp the crown of the plant with one hand, the pot with the other hand, and try to ease the plant from the pot. Do not pull it out. The idea is to loosen the root ball so it will slide from the container.

With very large containers, it is sometimes necessary to break the pot to avoid pulling out the plant and harming it. While this is not a very economical procedure, generally, after years of use, the pot is somewhat soiled or rotted and it is time to discard it anyway.

Place containers where you want them before you plant them. Large tubs and boxes filled with soil are heavy to move.

With a nursery-grown plant in a can, water it the day before planting. Slit the sides of the can (or have it done at the nursery) with a can cutter. Place the plant on its side on the ground and pry loose half of the can; then slide the plant out of the can. In a new container (or an old one washed and cleaned) cover the drain holes with shards or small stones or wire mesh and put in a bed of soil—about 3 to 4 inches, or more soil if it is a large box. Center the plant on the soil bed and fill in and around it with fresh soil. Press down to eliminate air gaps. Fill the pot with soil to within 1 or 2 inches of the rim. Soak the plant generously.

For balled or burlapped shrubs and trees, do not pick up the plant by the stem, but rather cradle the root ball in your hands and set it in place in the center of the prepared container. Fill in and around with soil until the container is about one half full. Soak with water, let settle a moment, and then add more soil. Before covering the crown of the plant, cut away the string that secures the burlap. It will rot away in time. Fill the pot to within 1 or 2 inches of the rim. Soak the plant generously.

Watering

Water indoor plants thoroughly and deeply and then allow them to dry out before watering them again. If possible, soak plants once a week in a tub of water for several hours or until the soil stops bubbling. This gives complete watering and keeps the root ball from drawing away from the container walls, causing a well. Remember that if soil becomes bone dry, the root ball shrinks and water runs down the sides of the pot, rather than into the roots.

Outdoor container plants need more frequent watering; they dry out faster than plants in the ground. Unless there is abundant rain, they need water almost every other day in warm weather. But watch them and learn their needs. In sunny windy times they will need more water than during cool cloudy days. Plants in unglazed containers dry out faster than those in wooden boxes. Large containers hold moisture longer than small ones, and plants close together shade one another and help to prevent excess moisture loss.

Do not allow soil to be constantly wet. It should be moist to the touch. Overwatering creates a soggy soil; the air is forced from the soil and plants suffocate or drown.

Occasionally—through neglect or circumstance—soil in large boxes becomes caked and it is impossible for water to penetrate it and get to the roots. Poke some holes in the soil. I hammer wooden stakes into the soil and then remove them. Then water can circulate to the plant roots.

Feeding

Some feeding is essential for container plants. Roots constantly take nutrients from the soil, and frequent watering leaches out food faster than we realize. Proper feeding keeps plants growing rather than merely living. But often people are anxious to see rapid growth and feed plants too much. There are times when fertilizing is beneficial and there are times when it can kill a plant.

Do not feed newly potted specimens for several weeks; there are adequate nutrients in fresh soil. Ailing plants and those resting should not be fed. The roots simply cannot absorb nutrients and will burn. In spring and summer, when plants grow rapidly, feed them every other watering. In fall and winter, when many of them rest, not at all.

Indoors, under less favorable conditions, plants do not grow fast and require less feeding than outdoor subjects. My house plants are fertilized only once a month in spring and summer, and not at all the rest of the year.

There are many plant foods, some specifically for roses or azaleas, other kinds for different plants. Liquids, powders, or pellets come in packages, cans, or bottles. Read the labels before selecting them and use the fertilizer that is most convenient for your purpose. All of them contain nitrogen, phosphorus, and potash in varying amounts in that order marked on the bottle or can. Nitrogen is an element that stimulates foliage growth, phosphorus promotes root and stem development and stimulates bloom, and potash stabilizes growth and intensifies color. Give foliage plants a high nitrogen fertilizer; flowering species need a formula with less nitrogen, because high concentrates of it can retard development of flower buds. I find a soluble fertilizer (10-10-5) the easiest to use and the best for most plants.

Maintenance and Care of Containers and Plants

I do not feed cacti or succulents, orchids or bromeliads. Through the years, I have found that these plants do better without feeding.

Preparations are now available for roses and other plants that feed and protect them from insects at the same time. These granules are scattered on the soil and water is applied over them.

Moving Containers

Large outdoor boxes and tubs are heavy; before putting them in place, provide adequate provisions for moving them. Newer

20. Jade trees in simple redwood boxes lead the guest to this house. (*Wimmer and Yamada, Landscape Architects; Photo by Douglas Simmonds*)

tubs and boxes are being built with handles, and this is indeed a convenience when you try to move them. Commercial units (boards and casters) called dollies are found at nurseries or, as mentioned previously, you can make them.

However, if you neglected to furnish a device for moving tubs or pots and must lift them, there are several old-fashioned methods that work. The easiest and best one is to use a skid cloth, or a burlap bag will be fine. Place the bag under the container, grab the other end, and start pulling it.

Another way to move heavy containers is to use lengths of 2-inch pipe. As the box moves over the pipes, take up one pipe from behind it and put it in front—not fast and not effortless, but this method succeeds, too, with push.

Do not, under any circumstances, try to pull a large container across the pavement. It scars the paving, and usually a wooden box comes loose at the corners under stress and strain.

Winter Storage

In climates where summers are short, provisions must be made for storing plants in winter. Their care and what to do with them varies with the area and the kinds of plant being grown.

Where temperatures go below zero, soil will freeze solidly and plants will die because they cannot get moisture. Remember that container plants in winter still need water, but if the soil freezes, wait for a thaw. Hardy evergreens like Japanese yew, hemlock, pine, and Douglas fir in large containers with plenty of soil will withstand some severe weather.

Where temperatures stay at freezing or a little below, say 26° F., rhododendrons, camellias, azaleas, firs, English and Korean boxwood, mahonia, and some euonymus species can be left outdoors. In sections where soil does not freeze, there is an even greater selection of plants—oleander, bougainvillea, aucuba, pittosporum, ficus, podocarpus, and so on.

House plants including ferns, palms, citrus, philodendron, and such must be moved indoors in early September in most areas. Many of the small or medium plants can be put in a sunroom or at a bay window to continue growing handsomely. Unheated, but not freezing, garages or porches are fine places for large tubbed plants. Many of them naturally rest in winter and need coolness (50° F.) and a shaded place. Keep them barely moist.

Where winters are severe, protect large concrete or glazed containers filled with soil. As soil freezes and thaws, it creates pressure against the sides and containers may crack. Remove the soil from them and cover the tubs and boxes with plastic or tarpaulin. The exception to this procedure would be the new Duraclay tubs that are guaranteed by the manufacturer to withstand freezing.

Pests and Diseases

If you follow a few simple rules, container plants will be relatively free of pests. Outdoors, hose them with a rather forcible stream of water about once a month. Indoors, give plants a good dousing under the shower (if possible) or at the sink under the faucet. Washing the foliage helps to keep plants free of insects and at the same time makes leaves shiny and handsome.

Remove infected or infested plants immediately before the pests spread to other plants. Isolate ailing ones that you suspect have disease or insects.

Inspect all new arrivals for insects. Soak the plants to the rim of the pot in a tub of water for about an hour. You will be surprised at the unwelcome guests that come to the surface of the soil.

Generally, outdoor plants in tubs and boxes are rarely bothered by insects. Ground crawlers simply do not make the trip up, let's say, and flying insects are easily washed away. And if your plants are elevated on blocks of wood—and they should be—the favorite hiding place of many insects is eliminated. Indoors, plants are perhaps more susceptible to pests. Dry air, overheating, and lack of fresh air make them more vulnerable to insect attack than outdoor plants.

Insecticides

Because there are so many insecticides—some control a number of pests, others fight a specific kind—know what you are fighting before you do battle. Inspect plants for leaf chewers—beetles, weevils, caterpillars, earwigs, snails, and slugs. Be on the lookout for sucking insects like aphids, mealybugs, spider mites, whiteflies, and scale.

Soil insects like cutworms, soil mealybugs, grubs, and so on cannot be seen, of course, and here it is a matter of removing the plant from its pot. When you determine the culprit, buy the control for it.

There are powders for dusting and liquids for spraying to help you help your plants. The most convenient kind of insecticide is a systemics type. This is applied as granules to the soil and then the plant is watered. One application will protect most plants (but not ferns or palms) from the majority of sucking and chewing insects for six to eight weeks.

Plant diseases—blight, canker, leaf spot—are treated with fungicides. Because diseases are rather rare in container plants, this section is purposely brief. To save an infected plant you must know the right time to apply the preventative and how to apply it properly. Read instructions on packages and cans and follow them diligently.

I keep a few insecticides on hand, infrequently used, I am happy to say. Most of them are for my outdoor plants. My indoor remedies, while old-fashioned, are still effective. I use soapy water (not detergents) for mealybugs, aphids, and whiteflies. When an indoor plant develops spider mites, I wash it every day in the sink until the mites disappear. I do have a house plant aerosol can (for all kinds of insects). I use it only when my simple remedies fail to rid the plants of insects.

Again let me say, use all insecticides only when absolutely necessary and strictly observe directions on the package. If in doubt, give less dosage than more. Be sure plants have been watered the day before applying chemicals. And keep them out of the sun for a few hours after using insecticides on them.

Most important, keep chemicals out of the reach of children and pets. I find a cabinet placed high on a wall a safe place for insecticides.

Insecticides
Malathion—for mealybugs, whiteflies, aphids.
Dimite—for spider mites.
Bug Getta or Cory's—for snails and slugs.

Fungicides
Karathane—for powdery mildew.
Zineb—for rose black spot, azalea blight.

Systemics
Isotox or Systox or Cygon—for most chewing and sucking insects.

Part Two
Container Gardening Outdoors

7. Painted wooden planters hold masses of color to decorate the side of a house. 8. A permanent brick planter is the feature of this patio court. (*Joyce R. Wilson photos*)

9. A lush display of petunias in a large window-box. (*Pan American Seed Co.*) 10. Hanging baskets of begonias and geraniums greet guests at this entrance. (*Joyce R. Wilson*) 11. Agapanthus fills this concrete-block permanent planter; an important display. (*Joyce R. Wilson*) 12. A glazed pot with a citrus plant is a bright accent to this stair area. (*Joyce R. Wilson*) 13. A shallow Duraclay planter for bulbs; red tulips are elegant in it. (*Architectural Pottery Co.*) 14. Graceful wistaria covers the small window-box complemented by a pot garden of orchids and geraniums at ground level. (*Joyce R. Wilson*)

15. A lovely garden accented with several container plants at varying levels. (*Molly Adams*) 16. A handsome cylindrical container filled with cascading petunias makes a perfect outdoor accent. (*Pan American Seed Co.*)

 *4. The Plants*

Almost any plant can be grown in a container temporarily, and many of them—camellias, for example—will thrive permanently in a box. The choice of plant material is limitless. New varieties like the Bonanza peach as well as stand-bys like palms and ferns are all likely candidates for pot gardening. Bromeliads, dramatic and carefree, do better in a tub than in the ground.

Trees and shrubs are necessary to balance the natural background of the outdoors. Strategically placed in tubs and boxes, they link the outdoor living area with the total setting. Vines are always welcome and give visual height and mass to an area; boxes of perennials and annuals and bulbs offer fresh color. Espalier and tree-form plants provide a note of elegance to the scene. And, of course, seasonal flowers in attractive pots are always desirable outdoors.

The placement and type of container must be considered. Boxes or tubs are well suited to patios or terraces or along a house wall. Or—properly placed—to accentuate walks and paths. Urns, jardinieres, and glazed pots are at their best near entrance and doorways. On top of a garden wall, these special containers are handsome too. A custom planter against a fence is another idea.

A group of different plants in pots—a pot garden—is especially appealing. It provides interest and color to otherwise barren areas. Even a few terra-cotta pots properly arranged add beauty.

Move plants around to achieve an attractive design; this is portable gardening and you are the decorator. Somewhat like arranging furniture in the home, placing container plants in the garden and patio requires discretion and thought.

As you select containers with care, also choose plants judiciously. Some of them, like palms and ferns, are tropical in appearance. Others, like podocarpus and camellias, are bold and dramatic, and still others—ficus and azara—are delicate and lacy. What you use depends on what kind of setting you want to create. The site, the character of the house, containers, and plants all have a part in a beautiful portable garden.

Trees and Shrubs

Small trees are basic container subjects. They offer some shade and provide visual background. The relationship of the tree and its tub must be considered. A 4-foot tree would be minimum for a 24-inch container. This gives a satisfying balance. Square or rectangular boxes are best for trees with bold foliage, while a lacy leaved Japanese maple looks best in the graceful curved outlines of a round container.

Small trees at nurseries come in 5-, 10-, and 15-gallon cans. Decide whether you want a fast-growing or a slow-growing kind. If you are not in temperate all-year climate, consider where the tree will go in winter. Some of them can be placed in a sunny window, others in an unheated but not freezing garage or porch. Even a basement with a little light is a place to store some plants.

Where shrubs are used, the relationship between the plant and the container should be about equal. Large terra-cotta

21. Trees and shrubs in border bed make this terrace an inviting place, a green haven in crowded city conditions. (*Molly Adams*)

pots, with lip or without detailing, are fine for shrubs. For plants like azaleas and geraniums with little significant height, a low container—a concrete bowl, perhaps—is best. Or use three-legged pots.

In climates with severe winters where there is no indoor space for plants, select hardy trees and shrubs for your area. The degree of hardiness of trees and shrubs is difficult to determine. Each section of the country has its own definition. However, there are certain plants that are considered hardy where temperatures go well below freezing. These trees and shrubs are marked with an asterisk in the following lists.

TREES

Acer palmatum (Japanese maple). A slow-growing tree with lacy leaves. It is handsome in soy tubs or in round containers. Needs protection from wind. Nice accent near doorways or in entrance court.

Araucaria excelsa (Norfolk Island pine). A lovely pyramidal shape; amenable plant. Can grow to 7 feet. Good vertical feature for deck or terrace.

Betula populifolia (gray birch). Deciduous; generally irregular in shape. Fine patio tree or good along house wall.

Cedrus atlantica glauca (blue atlas cedar). Needle evergreen with wide sprawling habit. Makes fine accent in large tubs near house corners.

Crataegus oxyacantha pauli (Paul's scarlet hawthorn). Deciduous; round-topped colorful tree. Good terrace feature.

Citrus (orange, lemon, lime). Many kinds offered. Dark green leaves and nice branching growth. Excellent in tubs, can be used anywhere.

Eriobotrya japonica (loquat). A round-headed tree with leathery dark green leaves. Nice full shape for tub or box. A row of these against a wood fence is handsome.

Ficus benjamina. Tiny dark green leaves, branching habit. Takes abuse and still grows well. For a special accent in the garden.

* *Ginkgo biloba* (ginkgo). Deciduous, irregular-shaped tree when young. Quite handsome in container; nice accent near a house wall.

* *Laburnum watereri* (golden-chain tree). Deciduous, with handsome columnar shape. Good patio feature.

Lagerstroemia indica (crape myrtle). A deciduous slow-growing tree with pink flowers. Needs full sun and summer warmth to prosper. A showy one for the patio.

Laurus nobilis (Grecian laurel). A compact tree with a

* denotes hardy plants

54

broad trunk, often several trunks to a tree. Slow growing with dark green leaves. Good for screening.

Magnolia soulangeana (saucer magnolia). Deciduous, with handsome round form; lovely flowers. For along a fence or wall.

Magnolia stellata (star magnolia). Deciduous round-topped tree with spectacular flowers. Good patio decoration.

Malus sargenti (sargent crab apple). Dwarf; fast grower with handsome round-topped form. Perimeter decoration for paved area.

Phellodendron amurense (cork-tree). Deciduous; attractive branching tree. For a special place.

Phoenix loureiri (date palm). Slow growing, well suited to tub culture. Has lovely arching fronds. An indoor-outdoor favorite.

Pinus mugo mughus (mugo pine). A popular patio standby. Irregular outline, broad and spreading. To decorate paths, walks, and patios.

Pinus parviflora glauca (Japanese white pine). Needle evergreen with horizontal-type growth. Nice feature in and around garden.

Pinus thunbergi (Japanese black pine). Good spreading habit; excellent container plant.

Podocarpus gracilior. Graceful willowy branches with needle-like leaves. Good doorway plant.

Rhapis excelsa (lady palm). Deep green fan-shaped leaves; a stellar container plant. Good on patio.

Salix matsundana tortuosa (contorted Hankow willow). Deciduous; lovely sweeping branches. For a special place.

Scheffera actinophylla (Australian umbrella tree). Graceful stems tipped with fronds of leaves. Will take abuse. Good patio performer.

Flowering cherry and apricot trees are other suggestions for tub growing, and the Bonanza peach and new hybrid tomato deserve special mention. They have been specifically bred for compact growth in tubs.

SHRUBS

Abutilon (flowering maple). Bell-shaped flowers of paper-thin texture. Many colors available; amenable plants that need plenty of water and sun.

*Arborvitae. Versatile evergreens that do well in containers. Many kinds.

*Azalea. Always welcome in the portable garden with brilliant flowers and lush growth. Keep them moist.

Camellia japonica. Excellent container plants in a profusion of colorful blooms. Many varieties.

Carissa grandiflora. Pretty white flowers and red plum fruit make this one desirable. Nice growth habit too.

*Cotoneaster. Glossy leaves and colorful berries. Plants are small or large; many possibilities.

Fatsia japonica (aralia). Handsome foliage specimen with fan-like leaves on tall stems. Makes bold appearance.

*Gardenia jasminoides. A lush shrub with dark green leaves and fragrant white blooms. Needs care—acid soil, protection from spider mites, and a soil that is moist at all times. Worth the trouble when you see a well-grown plant in bloom.

Hibiscus rosa-sinensis (Chinese hibiscus). Dark glossy green foliage; flowers single or double in a wide range of color. Give sun and plenty of water. Good performers in boxes or tubs.

Ilex crenata (Japanese holly). Many good species in this group, some hardy, others tender. Check with local nursery.

Ixora (star flower). A good evergreen shrub that blooms over a long period. Needs plenty of sun and water. Splendid color in white pots.

*Juniperus communis depressa (prostrate juniper). Good spreading plant with blue-green foliage. Forms dense mass.

J. chinensis pfitzeriana (pfitzer juniper). Makes an excellent screening plant. Not as hardy as prostrate juniper.

Nerium oleander (oleander). Graceful with dark green

* denotes hardy plants

leaves and cheerful flowers. Many colors—white, red, pink. Needs big container and buckets of water.

Osmanthus ilicifolius (holly olive). Glossy leaves on upright stems. Grows fast.

Pittosporum tobira. Graceful with arching branches and dark green leaves. Can be trained to shape.

Plumbago auriculata (Cape plumbago). Survives almost any situation. Small leaves and blue flowers for many months.

Podocarpus macrophylla. Bright green leaves; makes attractive tub plant.

Rhododendron. In boxes, these plants cannot be beat for outdoor decoration. Many varieties offering an incredible choice of flower color. Give them a good drainage and a slightly acid soil.

*Roses. All kinds and colors, and they do grow well in containers. Floribundas and hybrid teas good choices. Must have sun and good air circulation. Use complete fertilizer in spring and after blooming. Soak well every few days in spring and summer. Where hardiness is questionable ask you local nurseryman.

Viburnum. A good group with attractive leaves and pretty flowers followed by colorful berries. Many kinds. Need little care.

Yucca aloifolia (Spanish bayonet). Dramatic with blue-green sword-shaped leaves. Grows well in tub or box.

Vines

Any vine or trailer can be grown in a container. Their lush foliage and decorative habit of growth make them indispensable outdoor plants. Trained properly, they will cascade over fences and walls with a fountain of color. They can also be grown on trellises to afford privacy and to shield an unsightly view.

In many cases, where a paved surface of a driveway, or walk, or patio runs into a wall or a fence, a tubbed vine is the only way to complete the over-all garden. Any area looks better with a few vines in strategic places.

Prune and train vines to specific designs to create compositions that are handsome. According to their growth habits, a suitable support must be selected for vines. Few of them grow well or are handsome without a trellis or wood grid. They become vagrant and lose their vine characteristics. Although vines can be a problem when grown in the ground in the garden, in containers where roots are confined they do not choke off other plants.

The trellis or support must be sturdy to hold the weight of the plant. The top weight of a tall growing vine is best carried by a rafter or other substantial piece of structure. Metal-frame lattices are good. So are heavy-duty wooden ones. And there are special nails and other attaching devices at nurseries.

If you are covering a long fence, square redwood containers at the bottom of the fence, spaced equidistant from each other, are better than one gigantic tub. A vine in a planter at the bottom of a masonry wall will add interest to the wall; it is a good starting place for many vines.

When there are posts in the outdoor area, vines offer natural decoration. A tub of bougainvillea at the base of a post gives a colorful accent—much nicer than looking at bare wood. If you want color against the house or a pattern against white walls, start a large box of *cobaea scandens*. And at a doorway, vines make an entrance inviting.

In general, vines do not require special soil. Grow them in the same basic greenhouse mixture you use for other plants. Watering them depends on the climate and the amount of rain, and on the vine itself.

Here are some dependable vines:

Allamanda. Large yellow tubular flowers; big green leaves. Grows rapidly, clambers over an area, so train it carefully. Looks good in a corner against a house.

Bougainvillea. Magenta, purple, red, rose, pink, and white. A decorative vine that demands a "special" container. 'Fire King' and 'San Diego red' especially good. In winter, rest at 45° F.

Clematis. Known for attractive flowers. If you use large tubs you can enjoy the flowers close up. Quick growing. Many kinds available in lavender, pink, purple, and white. Needs sun, plenty of water. In autumn cut back the plant and place the tub in a cool place until growth starts again in spring. Hardy to 20° F.

Passiflora (passion vine). Odd flowers on a fast-growing vine. In North, treated as an annual. Many forms. Plants need large containers and a rich soil.

Plumbago auriculata. Not usually classified as a vine but does well when supported. Lovely blue flowers, lacy foliage. My choice for a small terrace wall or corner. Easy to grow. Hardy to 20° F.

Solandra guttata (cup-of-gold vine). Wide-spreading growth with broad leaves, golden yellow trumpet-shaped flowers. Needs full sun. Covers a large area. Tender.

Stephanotis. Wonderful scented white waxy flowers and glossy green foliage. Low growing but climbs easily; will not ramble. Good for low fences or spot wall decoration. Needs sunlight, plenty of water except in winter. Not hardy in the North. Keep in cool place in winter and water sparingly.

Trachelospermum jasminoides (star jasmine). A twiner with glossy green leaves, small white fragrant flowers. Needs a large pot or tub. Grows in sun or shade. Remove to indoors in winter.

Annuals

Most of the commonly grown annuals are available at nurseries. They are ideal for pots because the roots are shallow. Container annuals add color to a terrace or garden without waiting, and with proper care they bloom over a long period. Low-growing annuals like petunias give stellar splashes of concentrated color. Tall ones like *celosia plumosa* are excellent where a vertical accent is needed—perhaps against a terrace wall or a fence. And a few pots of butterfly flowers (schizanthus), so floriferous, are charming on the patio or terrace.

For a real display I group several different annuals in a redwood box, perhaps a bouquet of balsam in the center surrounded by vivid blue lobelia. For fragrance, nicotiana in tapered bowls is tough to beat. With annuals it is possible to have a constant flow of color in boxes all summer.

Use a good general potting mix for annuals and feed them biweekly. Water them heavily on warm days and be sure they get some sunshine.

Annuals for pots, boxes, and planters:

Browallia speciosa. The amethyst flower has small violet white-throated flowers. Needs bright light and copious water. Blooms through spring and summer.

Cineraria. Lovely flowers—blue, purple, red, crimson, and white. Bloom freely in partial shade and coolness. Look best in low standard clay pots.

Impatiens. Many varieties with double flowers in pink, white, or lavender. Handsome in tubs or boxes. Give plants sunlight, feeding.

Lobelia. Vivid blue, also a pale blue variety. Summer through fall color. Whether in baskets or pots, these are excellent small plants.

Petunias. All kinds, all easy to grow. Bloom for months in a wide color range—white, purple, pink, lavender, red, and now a new yellow. Dwarf ones, trailing ones, and large ruffled varieties. Just give them sun and water and they bloom their heads off. For a really stunning effect, grow a mass of one variety in a large cube redwood container.

Primrose. Many species and varieties in pink or lavender or white. Nice for window-boxes, border decoration. These plants like some shade.

Perennials

Perennials include many favorite flowers for continuous summer color. Geraniums, tuberous begonias, and chrysanthemums are only a few of the many plants at seasonal time.

All perennials must have a rest period sometime during the year. Those that bloom in summer rest over the winter. The winter plants rest in summer, the season of bloom depends on your individual climate.

Acanthus mollis (Grecian urn plant). Large, with rosettes of dark green leaves and erect spikes of white and lilac flowers in green bracts. Blooms easily with little care; needs large tub.

Campanula isophylla (bellflower). Blue star-shaped flowers. Needs plenty of water and partial shade. A small plant, it requires an ornate container.

Chrysanthemum. Excellent for autumn, with many sizes and colors to choose from. Many flower as late as November. Pinch back plants in early part of season, be sure soil is always moderately wet. Sunshine is best, although some varieties bloom in partial shade. Chrysanthemums are well suited to low standard clay pots or white shallow bowls.

Geraniums. Lady Washington varieties. Dark green heart-shaped leaves. Pink or red or lavender or white flowers with and without markings. Garden geranium is *Pelargonium hortorum*. Round leaves with scalloped margins, often with color zone in center. Single or double flowers in shades of white or pink or red or salmon. Groups of potted geraniums around posts or at entrance door or to decorate terrace corners are indeed handsome. A very large low tub filled with many geraniums of the same color is equally attractive (see Special Section at end of book).

Hellebore. Several species. Christmas rose: *H. niger*. Lenten rose: *H. orientalis*. Both good for boxes and tubs.

Hosta (plantain lily). Big, with lush green leaves. A very

22. Planter boxes brimming with daffodils is a feature of this outdoor area. (*Photo by Mason Weymouth*)

Bulbs

Potted bulbs offer early spring color, a succession of bloom through many months, and they are lovely in appropriate pots and tubs.

Many spring bulbs can be planted in pots in late fall and stored over the winter in a cool dark shaded place—a basement, a pantry—and brought into the house in early winter. Leaves will be pale yellow and white from lack of light, but once at a bright warm window, foliage turns green and growth starts in a matter of days. In a few more weeks, when it is safely warm outside, move them to the terrace or patio.

After they flower, take the bulbs inside but don't cut off the foliage. Keep it growing until leaves begin to yellow. Then gradually let the soil dry out. When foliage and soil are dry, take the bulbs from the pots and store them in brown-paper sacks in a cool place for fall planting.

A good soil mix for bulbs is: 3 parts garden loam, 1 part sand, and 1 part leaf mold. For a concentration of color, plant bulbs close together. To start bulbs, cover the bottom of the container with pebbles. Fill the pot about one third full of soil and set the bulbs on top. Fill in and around until the tips are barely covered.

23. Iris plants in narrow redwood boxes can be used anywhere on the patio for color accent.

Achimenes. Pretty color from charming small plants. Although suitable for standard pots I prefer them in hanging baskets. Plants come in a variety of colors. All need sun, plenty of water.

Autumn *crocus.* Dramatic tulip-shaped flowers in brilliant yellow, lavender, or rose color. Several to a redwood box or shallow clay pot make a showy display in August and September. Grow them quite wet in partial shade. For contrast, set crocus in pots on brick floor or against paved walls.

Daffodils. Many varieties blooming from January to May. Most of the easy-to-grow ones sparkle with color in planters and window-boxes. Plant bulbs in late fall. When growth starts move them to sunshine. Keep them liberally watered.

Hyacinth. Much color for little effort. A hardy bulb with bright green leaves and fragrant flowers in white or pink or blue. Needs lots of sun, plenty of water. March and April blooming.

Kafir lily. Mature plants in pots are at nurseries in winter for spring bloom. Very dramatic with clusters of vivid orange or red flowers, the Kafir lily deserves a spot on the terrace. Looks grand in large round tubs and can be grown in the same container for several years.

Lilies. Excellent patio plants but their color does not last long enough for me. All kinds of lilies are available from summer to fall, depending upon varieties chosen.

Espaliers

If there is a wall in the garden that needs something special, or if you want a decorative accent against the house, try espaliers. Growing plants trained to patterns has advantages. They occupy a minimum of space, and where some shrubs in the ground may have vagrant growth, in a pot they stay neat and good-looking. They make an interesting background in the garden.

There are a number of espalier patterns: formal, informal, U-shaped, double U-shaped, horizontal, gridiron, free form, informal fan, braided tree. A tree or shrub used as an espalier needs help. Tie the branches where you want them. Keep the plant trained to the desired shape. Tying must be done constantly throughout the growing season. Branches too far out of line become difficult.

Provide a well-drained soil for espaliers and choose plants for appropriate conditions—sun lovers for a south wall, shade plants at a north or west exposure. Do not fertilize espaliers; too much nitrogen makes it impossible to keep plants to a desired shape.

CONTAINER-GROWN ESPALIERS

Camellias. Wonderful espalier plants; varieties in many colors and combinations of color—from white to pink to dark red. Good ones are 'Elegans,' 'Lady Clare,' and 'Bride's Bouquet.' Need partial shade and protection from the wind. Soil should be acid and evenly moist.

Citrus trees. Orange, lemon, grapefruit, and kumquat are excellent for espalier growing. In winter move them indoors to a sunny window.

Ficus carica. A deciduous shrub with 3 to 5 lobed leaves and pear-shaped fruit. It needs sun and an evenly moist soil.

Ilex crenata (Japanese holly). Broad-leaved evergreen shrub that needs shade and a rich well-drained soil.

Jasminum nudiflorum. Dark green leaves and yellow flowers.

Give the plant partial shade or sun and a light well-drained soil. Has a delicate appearance.

Magnolia grandiflora. Makes a stately pyramid. With handsome glossy green leaves and huge white flowers, it wants sun and a rich soil. Give it plenty of water.

Malus atrosanguinea. A small crab-apple tree with dark pink flowers. Needs sun, rich soil. Easy to grow in tubs.

Pyracantha coccinea 'lalandei.' Dark green leaves and white flowers. Masses of orange or red berries in winter. Takes sun or shade, rich well-drained soil. Can be easily trained.

Taxus baccata repandens. Needle evergreen shrub with arching branches. Give it bright light, rich well-drained soil.

24. An espalier camellia against a house wall. (*Joyce R. Wilson*)

Standards

Standards, or plants trained to tree form, have a sculptured quality that brings a note of elegance to the garden or patio. Many plants can be trained to grow as standards, but azaleas, fuchsias, and geraniums are perhaps best known.

You can train your own standards; this takes patience and skill. Or you can buy them in 5-gallon cans from a nursery and enjoy them immediately. Place standards where there is some protection from the wind.

Basically, all three plants mentioned above can be trained in the same manner. As growth starts pinch off side shoots, forcing activity to the top (leave a few small leaves on the stem). When the plant is about 12 inches high give it bamboo support. Tie the stem to the bamboo with plastic ties. Fertilize every other watering to encourage growth. Transfer the plant to an 8- or 10-inch pot and allow branches to develop at the tip.

Through the growing season maintain the proper ball shape and remove side shoots. In spring when the tree is in its second year, bloom starts.

Plants to train to tree form:

GERANIUMS

'Scarlet Flame'
'Lavender Richard'
'Masure's Beauty'
'Missouri'
'Orange Richard'
'Prize'

FUCHSIAS

'Carnival'
'Flying Cloud'
'Gypsy Queen'
'Pink Bountiful'
'Swingtime'

AZALEAS

'Falling Waters'
'George Tabor'
'Pink Fountain'

Basket Plants

The beauty of plants at eye level cannot be denied; they are easily seen and add color and interest to otherwise barren areas. In handsome containers, they complete the garden picture.

There are many trailers and climbers that can be used for baskets—some for flower, others for foliage. And there are dozens of containers to put them in (see Chapter 1).

Here are a few of the many plants for baskets:

Asparagus sprengeri (emerald fern). One of the choice trailers with feathery leaves and tiny white flowers followed by red berries.

Begonia tuberhybrida 'Pendula.' Cascades of colorful flowers; unbeatable summer color but difficult in parts of the country with hot summer weather. Need coolness and shade (see Special Section).

Campanula fragilis (bellflower). Small blue flowers and lush foliage make this a perfect basket plant. Needs only a little sun.

Fuchsia (lady's eardrops). Many fine trailers; easy plants in partial shade (see special section at end of book).

Geraniums (ivy-leaved). Many kinds (see Special Section).

Hedera (ivy). Pretty foliage plant that does well in shade.

Lantana montevidensis. A robust grower that blooms for months. Attractive lavender flowers.

Petunia (cascade varieties). Absolutely the finest annual for baskets. Many kinds; new varieties get bigger and better every year. Give sun.

Rosmarinus officinalis 'Prostratus' (rosemary). Not often seen but a fine creeping plant that cascades over the pot with dark green foliage and bright lavender flowers.

Tropaeolum majus (nasturtium). Bright and lovely; makes a big splash of color. Need sun.

25. Wall containers and bowls are part of this outdoor scene. (*Architectural Pottery Co.*)

Succulents and Cacti

This is a big family of plants with many overlooked gems that come to life in pots and tubs. Where something unusual is wanted, cacti and other succulents are tough to beat and easy to care for. Some of the big agaves and aloes are particularly desirable because of their leaf color—blue-green, purple-green—and their sculptural qualities.

26. A collection of succulents in striking white pots. (*Architectural Pottery Co., photo by Julius Shulman*)

Select mature plants; these are slow growers and, unlike other plants that require frequent watering, cacti and succulents can —if necessary—go without water for weeks.

Grow plants in a sandy soil or, if they are the jungle kind, in equal parts of fir bark and soil. You will need gloves to handle the spiny ones.

Where temperatures go below 40° F. in winter, plants must be moved indoors to an unheated, but not freezing, garage or porch or a sunny window. Remember that most cacti and succulents rest in winter and need lower temperatures, about 55° F., and little, if any, water.

These are some of the plants I grow:

Aeonium arboreum. Decorative rosettes on tall stems that appear like full-blown roses. Need almost no care.

Agave Americana marginata (century plant). Big spiny giant with sword-shaped leaves, yellow and green. Dramatic in the right container.

Agave attenuata. Big, bold, and full of color. Thrives in a tub for years.

Agave Victoriae reginae. Small but lovely globe of handsome olive-green leaves delicately penciled along the edges. Beautiful.

Crassula argentea (jade plant). Old favorite, with bright green leathery leaves. Nice tree form.

Dudleya brittonii. Big white rosettes of leaves. Striking display in white tub. Mature plants only.

Epiphyllum (orchid cactus). Superb flowers in May and June. Color range incredible, size mammoth. Don't let the

27. Birds-of-paradise are a colorful feature in redwood box on this deck.

sprawling growth habit of the plant scare you away from them. They can be staked to grow vertically. Many varieties. I've yet to see a bad one.

Euphorbia grandicornis. An oddity, with branching stems armed with heavy spines.

Kalanchoe tomentosa (panda plant). Long tapering leaves covered with hair, edges dark brown. Unusual. Pot in equal parts of fir bark and soil.

Zygocactus (Christmas cactus). Another superb flowering group with many varieties, some of them making a solid ball of color. Grow in equal parts of fir bark and soil.

28. Pots of bromeliads are sunk in the ground for this appealing pool picture. (*Author photo*)

Bromeliads

Bromeliads are plants with incredible leaf color and bright gaudy flowers. Many of them are rosettes, others tubular or vase shaped. Some are medium size, others giants, but all of them are easy to grow and add a lot of color to an area for little cost.

Bromeliad care is simple. Most of them have a bowl or vase formation of leaves. Keep the base filled with water; that is all there is to it. Pot bromeliads in equal parts of shredded fir bark and soil.

Here are some dependable species, all of which require a minimum night temperature of 45° F.

Aechmea chantini (Silver King). To 40 inches, variegated vase-shaped plant; red and yellow flowers. Need some sun.

Billbergia venezuelana. A giant with broad leaves and mosaic patterns of chocolate brown with silver bands. Needs large tub and some sun. A real spectacle in bloom.

Guzmania monostachia. To 30 inches; satiny green leaves in a rosette. Tall flower spike with white flowers and green bracts, tipped red. Will take shade; handsome in white pot.

Hohenbergia ridleyi. To 5 feet, with golden-yellow leaves and a tall branched yellow-and-red flower head. Cannot be beat as accent plant on patio.

Pitcairnia carolina. To 36 inches; tubular growth. Incredible red flowers.

Portea petropolitana var. extensa. To 48 inches, fan-shaped growth. Lush green leaves and multicolored flower spike. Needs sun and large tub.

Streptocalyx poeppiggi. To 48 inches; a dense rosette of spiny leaves. Whitish rose flowers. Needs bright light.

Vriesia fenestralis. To 40 inches; green leaves delicately figured with darker green and lined purple. Big and bushy. Ideal for wooden box. Also handsome is V. *hieroglyphica* with rosettes of light green, crossbanded with dark green. These are favorite landscape plants in South America.

Orchids

Orchids are splendid plants no more difficult to grow than ferns or palms and perhaps easier to tend to. The orchid flower is well known and outstanding in the plant world. More and more, these are becoming popular plants for indoor and outdoor decoration.

The majority of orchids are epiphytic (growing on trees) or, some, terrestrial (growing in the ground). The epiphytes must be potted in fir bark or osmunda (at nurseries). It is imperative that water does not linger at the roots of plants, so be sure drainage is perfect when planting orchids.

Containers—open slatted baskets, strawberry jars—that permit air to circulate around the roots are best for these plants. If they are in standard pots be sure to make arrangements for bottom ventilation. Orchids will not thrive in pots set directly on the floor. Use florist wire stands or make wooden platforms for them. The idea is for air to circulate around the base of the pot.

Some species need a great deal of sun, others will bloom in bright light. Most of them do not tolerate temperatures below 55° F.

These orchids listed here are spring and summer blooming. There are also fall and winter flowering species.

Ansellia africana gigantea. To 40 inches. Delightful patio orchid with cane growth and evergreen leathery leaves. Bright yellow and brown flowers in summer. Grow in fir bark. Give sun and warmth.

Bletilla hyacinthina. Low growing to 16 inches. Good in small boxes; bright lavender flowers. Grow in equal parts of soil and fir bark. Need scattered sun.

Coelogyne massangeana. To 36 inches. Decorative broad leaves and pendent spikes of small beige and brown flowers. An easy one to grow in coolness and shade. Pot in fir bark.

Cymbidium. Many varieties available that grow lavishly in tubs. Need cool nights (45° F.) while setting buds in fall.

Dendrobium moschatum. Dark green leaves and glamorous beige and maroon flowers in spring. Needs cool nights in winter (45° F.) to set buds. Grow in fir bark.

Epidendrum o'brienianum. Grows to 60 inches. Reed-like stems crowned with bunches of tiny red flowers. Needs sun; grows in fir bark.

Phaius grandifolius (nun's orchid). To 40 inches with big broad decorative leaves and large multicolored flowers. Grows in equal parts of soil and fir bark.

Rhynchostylis gigantea. Strap-like leaves to 30 inches. Bears pendent scapes of small white flowers, spotted red. Pot in fir bark. A stellar display in bloom.

Sobralia leucoxantha. To 48 inches. Dark green paper-thin leaves and 4-inch rose-purple flowers. Dramatic. Grow in equal parts of soil and fir bark.

5. Containers in Place

Patios and terraces need container plants to make them inviting. And bare areas such as paved walks and walls, fences, entryways, house walls, and corners near the building also need decoration. A few pot plants immediately make an area attractive.

Special places like loggias and lanais, atriums and solariums are other places that require plants and containers. They become an integral part of the area and must be chosen carefully.

Patio and Terrace

A patio or terrace simply is not furnished without container plants. It is like a room without furniture. A few small trees in tubs, a well-chosen shrub in a decorative pot create balance with the outdoor landscape. Boxes of annuals or perennials add color; pots of bulbs provide fragrance. Scale, too, is important, and plants must have a similar character of largeness or smallness to correspond to house and surroundings.

To provide adequate growing space and have plants where

you want them, boxes and planters and decorative tubs are necessary. You can buy them or make them yourself. If you are in areas where summers are short, simply slip potted plants in large boxes or planters and fill in and around them with sphagnum moss. Then it is easy to move them indoors in winter. Planters can be portable or built in place as benches or retaining walls if necessary.

Boxes and planters can be used effectively to make grid patterns on the patio or they can be placed against the house in a corner, or in groups around posts. Even a row of four small boxed trees at the outer edge of a patio gives height and focus to the area. On a narrow terrace, the trees can be placed against the house wall.

Portable boxes with plants can line a driveway, conceal unsightly areas, direct traffic, protect low-growing plants, or frame an existing shrub or tree. There are limitless possibilities for container plantings outdoors.

The beauty of this kind of gardening is not only in the plants and flowers; they can be moved about to perform many functions.

Walks and Paths

Long expanses of paved walks and paths that lead to the garden or house are monotonous. A few well-chosen container plants make them interesting. Do not use large bushy specimens —this would obstruct the walk—but select plants like tulips and daffodils that are vertical and do not interfere with traffic.

A handsome plan is a large Italian pot at one end of the path punctuated by an identical container at the other end of the walk. Colorful annuals make a handsome display.

If the path runs along a house wall, narrow redwood boxes filled with colorful annuals bring interest and brightness to the area. Planting pockets bordered with brick or redwood break up a long walk and are lovely with ground cover or trailing plants.

If you have colored paving, select appropriate contrasting-color containers. A path does not have to be a bare strip; with container plants it is part of the garden.

Garden Walls

Garden and terrace walls, whether used for protection from the wind or for decoration, are ideal places for potted plants, or the base of the wall for espalier trees in tubs. Star jasmine, clematis, or any climbing vine can be grown. The tree against the wall gives it interest and adds charm to the setting.

Sculptural plants like New Zealand flax or some agaves are dramatic against a brick or stone wall and relieve the monotony of the masonry. If it is a retaining wall, sink a trough in it filled with junipers, or if you prefer flowers, try Indica azaleas.

Put small pots on the wall, large tubs where there are low broad ledges. Trailing ivy geraniums, fuchsias, and weeping lantana are stunning cascading over the bricks. Even a few pots of heliotrope or geranium make a wall more than a barrier.

If you do not want to use plants at the base of the wall but would rather have them at different levels on the surface of the wall, this is possible too. Clip-on hangers (available at nurseries) can be placed anywhere on a wall; they hold pots by the rim with a clasping device.

Doorway and Stairs

Stairs are for walking, but they are for pot plants, too, if they do not interfere with foot traffic. A few small containers can be at the top or the base of the stairs, or if there is a banister, a row of pots at varying levels leading to the stairway is desirable. If it is a wide stairway, containers, perhaps 10 inches square, can be made to fit the edge of the steps. Filled with geraniums, this is a colorful border to lead guests to the door.

Doorways are other places for container plants. Generally, there is a slab or an elevated pedestal. A large tub with a geranium or rose tree near the door makes an elegant entrance. Or concrete tubs with lush foliage plants to frame a doorway

29. Evergreens in Spanish pots accent this wood-brick patio. (*Ken Molino*) 30. A Japanese maple in a redwood box is part of this deck-patio setting. (*California Assn. of Nurserymen*) 31. A poolside planting of cyperus with pots sunk in ground. (*California Assn. of Nurserymen*)

are a welcoming sight. A pair of plants to decorate an entrance, one on each side, is handsome too.

Where there is a niche, this is an ideal spot for a pedestal urn brimming with geraniums or tuberous begonias, or use twin tubs of chrysanthemums for seasonal color beside an entry. If a touch of drama is desired, try spear-leaved yuccas in tubs.

Plants look good at doorways whether in pairs or as single specimens. Why have a bare entrance, when you can make it appealing with a few potted plants?

Penthouse and Rooftop Gardens

The garden in the sky is generally small and needs intensive decoration to make it attractive. Unique tubs and boxes can quickly convert these areas into gardens. Each plant—an espalier tree or shrub, a weeping birch, cascading tuberous begonias— should be selected to achieve dramatic beauty. This is more a showplace garden than a working garden, and the rooftop greenery is badly needed in the midst of crowded city living.

Because these gardens are small, it is best to make an over-all plan on paper. Design and architectural accent are important. On patios and terraces there is room to move things around. On roof gardens, each container is worth its weight, let's say, because weight must be given special consideration. It is a good idea to check with your building superintendent to determine how much weight you can safely put on the roof. The matter of drainage is also important; the surface of the roof must be in a watertight condition. Usually, the rooftop will already have a coat of asphalt or tar and gravel, but be sure there are no cracks where water may seep through the roof surface. Excess water must also drain freely and be channeled away via gutters and downspouts. Be sure these devices are in place and in good condition.

For penthouse gardens, choose trees for height and scale to balance the area, evergreen shrubs for year-round beauty. Vines soften wall lines, hide unsightly places, and since a rooftop garden is generally walled, vines take on special importance. Flowering plants for color and fragrance are necessary too.

Basically, the same containers for patios and terraces are good for rooftop gardens—tubs, urns, redwood boxes, tapered bowls, wine casks—and glazed ceramic tubs can be used for a focal point. Each object is a showpiece. Seek unusual containers; do not be content with just common ones. The roof garden is special, so it should have some flair.

32. A strawberry jar with miniature roses greets guests at this doorway garden. (*Star Roses photo*)

33. A penthouse-roof garden with raised planter beds and column of standard clay pots framing the area. (*Molly Adams*)

Try fruit trees such as apple and pear. A willow tree is another suitable choice; it does well in the city. The Japanese maple is another good candidate; it is decorative and withstands wind better than most trees. Evergreen magnolias are handsome where mass is needed, and shrubs like azaleas and camellias in protected corners are a touch of magic. Shady places are for fuchsias and begonias, and oleanders and gardenias need a sunny spot. Tree roses in planting boxes bring elegance to the rooftop garden.

Today, many people are successfully growing vegetables in containers. Ordinary clay pots will do, but choose large ones (14 or 16 inches in diameter). Vegetables that respond well to container culture are sweet and hot peppers, cucumbers, and tomatoes. Put these pot gardens in sun and keep soil well watered at all times. You will not be able to feed your entire family with these vegetable gardens, but it is fun indeed just to have a little fresh produce you have grown yourself.

A word here about the hazards of rooftop gardening. Wind protection might be necessary, and while it is undesirable to enclose all sides of the garden there should be one protected corner. Use louvered boards or grid-type fencing to break the wind without cutting off the passage of air.

Noon sun brings intense heat to rooftop plants; place pergolas and awnings strategically to provide shade for plants and man. Also, plants will get their share of smoke and soot, so hose them down frequently to keep them healthy.

Today, many apartments have small balconies and, tiny though they may be, these areas can be lovely sky gardens. A few seasonal pot plants add color to the balcony, and a small tree in a handsome tub is always charming. Balcony gardens, like rooftop retreats, can be decorated with the same kind of plants mentioned earlier in this section. And of course include vines to cover walls with fresh green and also to provide vertical accent.

Don't hang pots on railings or set them on ledges; wind can knock them over. Use wall brackets for plants for the house wall of the balcony, and start climbers in shallow boxes at the base of guard fences. Even in one season many vines such as *cobaea scandens* or clematis will cover the barrier.

Pond and Pool

A reflecting pond with an expanse of water is a natural place for container plants. They enhance the water area and complete the picture. A lush green frame of plants is attractive and demands attention.

Handsome, graceful ferns are best for pond areas, but foliage specimens like plantain lily and cast-iron plant are good too. Use groups of pots with airy plants for that fresh green look. The natural requirements of primulas and marsh marigolds that flourish in moist conditions are other fine choices. Asparagus fern, dripping lacy green fronds, is equally at home around the reflecting pond. New Zealand flax in a squatty tub with sculptural leaves demands attention; try the red-bronze variety for a bright spot.

Tall vertical plants with arching stems and diminutive leaves provide moving shadows on the water surface, forever interesting with its changing designs. A small weeping beech or maple in a white tub by the water is a scene worth sharing with others.

The shape and size of the pond dictate the kind of containers to use. Tubs are best for round or irregular-shaped pools. They accentuate the design and show off the foliage to the best advantage. Glazed white tubs and urns are effective, and better than wooden containers for a water setting; large terra-cotta tapered bowls are another possibility.

Perhaps we should here mention water lilies and lotus. Their beauty is well known, and now several miniature varieties are available for container growing. You will need a large water-tight tub (at least 12 inches in diameter and 14 inches deep). Keep the water garden in a sunny place and enjoy the exotic flowers in July and August. Water plants are available from several suppliers and are shipped in April or May. Give plants more soil than ordinary plants and feed them every other week. Most lilies need at least 4 inches of water above the crown of the plant.

Part Three
Container Gardening Indoors

6. Miniature Gardens

There is a special appeal in all things miniature, and the tiny garden—in a dish or a bottle or dwarf plants in containers—is no exception. Here we really see the plant, and each one takes on importance it would not have in larger-scale paintings.

Lilliputian landscapes have advantages too. Only a small amount of soil is needed, and care is at a minimum once the planting is established. Tiny gardens can be planted in any container of stone, iron, wood, or earthenware. The containers can be large or small but they should be at least 4 to 5 inches deep. These gardens occupy little space, and even apartment dwellers can have pleasure from miniature gardens.

Hundreds of tiny plants are available, from roses to native specimens, and each diminutive landscape has its own charm. The dish garden is always effective when used to accent a table or bench. The bottle garden intrigues both children and adults. The fine art of bonsai has legions of followers. It merely becomes a matter of choice, and, truly, it is little trouble to have a garden of each kind.

Gardens can be simple with only house plants or they can

be elaborate with alpine and rock plants in stone sinks and troughs. Bog gardens with fascinating insectivorous plants can be grown in closed containers—they do not live in pots on sills —and even natural containers of slag or tufarock with appropriate plantings are unique.

Dish Gardens

Any group of living plants in an interesting container without a cover is a dish garden. A few potted plants lined up on a window sill simply do not have the appeal of a group of well-chosen plants in a glass garden or in a dish.

Each garden can be a scene—a miniature replica of nature—whether it be woodland, oriental, or tropical in theme. And do decide on a dominant theme for the garden rather than having it a hodgepodge of plants. Because the dish garden is a diminutive setting, each plant is important to the whole. Miniature compositions are always more difficult to create because they are under closer scrutiny than large-scale ones. The garden must be distinctive and created with care. Plants and containers should be chosen with thought; this is a product of your imagination.

A successful dish garden requires some skill and talent to create the pleasing picture, the harmony and balance of plants, container, and textures.

There is no set rule about the size or shape of the container. It can be round, square, rectangular, or elliptical but it must be deep enough for at least 4 inches of soil. Search for an interesting container rather than a commercial one. Glass lamp shades, teacups, coffee cups, soufflé dishes, soup bowls, fluted baking dishes, and such can be used. Or have a simple metal pan or a galvanized tray in a woven bread basket or a rattan bowl. Match the plant to the container. That is, in the fluted dish grow bold round-leaved plants. In a teacup, plant the charming miniature gloxinia and baby-tears. For a large white bowl, try cacti and succulents with round sculptural leaves.

Place gardens in any room in the house, in any place—a

bedside table, a mantel, a coffee table, in a bookcase shelf, or perhaps on a window sill. To protect surfaces from moisture stain use decorative table mats. (I water dish gardens at the sink and let them drain a few minutes; even so; there is always some moisture seepage later.)

Miniature gardens are for accent; they are like pictures on the walls to decorate a room. Do not fret if they do not last a lifetime—they will outlast a dozen roses or a gift plant and usually cost much less. However, if you happen to be penurious like me and want them to last a long time, keep them near windows where they have light.

34. The desert-theme dish garden has been popular for many years. (*Roche photo*)

Putting the Garden Together

Before you start a dish garden, place the potted plants in the container and move them around until you hit on the right placement. If you buy plants only in 2- or 3-inch pots— and you should—this is a simple procedure. Set the largest plant to one side of the dish—never in the center—to create an accent, and put small plants around the base.

For a striking effect, use the accent plant in a bed of white sand or colored gravel.

Trim plants so they have a sculptural growth. For instance, *punica granatum* 'Nana' (dwarf pomegranate) is a fine dish garden subject; it can be pruned to the desired shape without harming it. Use bold foliage plants like peperomias against the graceful fronds of a fern, a feathery yellow-green *asparagus sprengeri* (emerald fern) in front of a dark green bold plant like *kalanchoe blossfeldiana*.

A flat design with level grading of earth is dull; use hills and valleys. Shape the contour of the soil so that it is interesting and pleasing. Make the front of the garden low and mound the soil in the rear. Set a plateau of soil and pieces of flat shale in a corner. There are many variations; use some imagination.

Select the appropriate soil for the plants being grown. Here is my standard potting mix for most plants:

1 part garden loam
1 part sand
1 part leaf mold

As mentioned under "Maintenance and Care of Containers and Plants," I add more sand to this mix for succulents and cacti, more loam for moisture-loving plants like ferns and mosses. For miniature bromeliads and orchids I use a pocket of fir bark.

A word about packaged mixes; while they may be suitable for some plants they are often too muddy for many plants. Be sure the mix is porous and has an open texture.

To start the dish garden, tease the plants from their individual containers—don't pull them out—and set them in place. Arrange and rearrange until you are satisfied with their positions. Firm the soil around the collar of the plant to support it. Put in trailers and ground covers last. Water the garden so the soil is just moist but don't set it in sun. Wait a few days before setting the container in light.

Try to keep the soil evenly moist at all times; this is not an easy matter. What looks moist on top may be bone dry at the bottom. I poke my finger deep into the soil, trying not to dislodge any plants, to test for moisture. Then I know if I should water the garden.

Never dump water into the dish, for you will dislodge plants and soil. Pour water gently from a spout can.

Spray foliage regularly to keep it dust free and fresh. Pick off faded flowers and dead leaves. Keep the piece attractive. If plants are getting straggly and unattractive, trim them ruthlessly. I have no qualms about doing this; most house plants are tough and recover quickly with fresh new growth. Fragile though they may seem, I can assure you that plants want to live.

Generally, living-room temperatures are fine for dish gardens; namely; 72–80° F. during the day, 62–72° F. at night.

Plants

A multitude of miniature plants and seedlings of mature ones can be used for gardening in dishes. Most of them are at florist shops; others are mail-order subjects. There are trees, flowering plants, foliage gems, even water plants. Most certainly, select plants that grow slowly and choose species that are compatible; ferns and mosses need a rich soil and shade. Flowering plants require a few hours of daily sun and a standard soil, while desert plants like some crassulas and cacti need a sandy soil and quite a lot of sun. One of my objections to florists' dish gardens—lovely though they may be—is that too often they do not contain compatible plants. A few species will

95

thrive in the sun while other plants will die; the result is a garden that must be done over. And by all means, do not crowd plants; give them room to grow.

As mentioned, select a theme for the garden. Then it is easy to create a harmonious pleasing arrangement. While there are many different kinds of gardens—rustic, informal, formal, and so on—the tropical, woodland, oriental, and desert settings are most popular. Here are some suggestions:

Tropical Garden

Here is where you can use all kinds of small plants that like warmth (78° F. by day, ten degrees cooler at night) and partial sunlight (about three hours a day). Try to create a lush effect but do not crowd the scene. Use creeping ground cover and miniature ferns, orchids, and bromeliads. The terrain should be hilly rather than flat, and this garden is better assembled without figurines or props. Use a standard soil mix except for bromeliads and orchids that will need osmunda or fir bark.

Suggested plants for the tropical garden:

Allophytum Mexicanum
Carissa grandiflora
Chamaeranthemum venosum
Euonymous japonicus microphyllus
Kalanchoe pumila
Leptotes bicolor
Malpighia coccigera
Masdevallia simula
Oncidium pullchelum
Punica granatum 'Nana'
Rex begonias (miniatures)
Tillandsia ionanthe

Woodland Garden

This is a popular scene, always fresh and inviting and es-

35. Here the woodland theme is represented in an aquarium. (*Roche photo*)

pecially cheerful on gray winter mornings. Native plants are usually suggested for this setting, but because they sometimes are difficult to get, house plants and allied species can be used.

In this garden, you can be somewhat quaint in your selections. Use a rather large container like a baking dish or a shallow casserole. Plan hills and valleys and if you want sow some grass seed. Search for dwarf trees (from bonsai suppliers) or use seedlings. Average living room temperature and 50 per cent humidity with about three hours of sunlight will make these plants thrive in the woodland garden:

Acorus gramineus variegatus
Azalea 'Gumpo'
Begonia aridicaulis
Cryptanthus acaulis
Cryptanthus zonatus
Echeveria glauca
Hedera helix 'Glacier'
Kalanchoe 'Tom Thumb'
Neanthe bella
Oxalis hedysaroides rubra
Pellaea rotundifolia
Pilea depressa
Saxifraga sarmentosa
Sempervivum arachnoideum
Sinningia pusilla

Oriental Garden

Simplicity is the keynote of this setting. The very nature of the theme—sparse beauty—means that just one feature out of proportion to the whole will ruin the garden. Stones, mosses, and figurines must be selected with care, and the container chosen should be special. Use only a few plants and leave space for a path. For a tree, select an upright plant with a single stem that is attractively shaped. Grow a few strands of grass that appear like bamboo.

Plant selections for the oriental theme:

Acorus gramineus variegatus
Begonia dregei
Begonia 'Lulandi'
Gasteria lilliputana
Laelia pumila
Punica granatum 'Nana'
Sedum multiceps
Tillandsia ionanthe

Desert Garden

These landscapes of cacti and succulents need plenty of sun, warmth, and a sandy soil. Use a container of any shape but deep enough for 4 inches of soil. Keep the soil rather dry, never wet. Put in a few white marble chips for color and perhaps an interesting small stone for contrast. In most cases, do not expect flowers, but the interesting shapes and growth of desert plants make them desirable. These gardens can remain in the same container for several years without replacing the plants.

Succulent plants for the desert setting:

Adromischus maculatus
Astrophytum myriostigma
Crassula schmidti
Crassula teres
Gasteria lilliputana
Haworthia tessellata
Monanthes polyphylla
Portulacaria afra variegata
Rhipsalis mesembryanthoides
Sedum dasyphyllum

Bottle Gardens and Terrariums

The garden in glass—in a bottle or a terrarium—has advantages. Within the confines of a glass container there is a moist atmosphere and plants are protected from drafts. Moisture condensing on the glass helps to water the soil, humidity is at a high level, and the glass garden practically takes care of itself. Small ferns and other moisture-loving plants that generally would not survive window sill conditions thrive. Even some miniature orchids can be grown successfully.

The first terrarium was probably the Wardian case invented by Nathaniel Ward, a London physician, about a hundred years ago. Today, terrariums include brandy snifters, tobacco jars, rose bowls, candy dishes, pickle jars, and so on.

36. Preparing sheet moss to line a brandy snifter. Drainage material, soil, and plants will be added in that order to complete the pretty picture. (*Roche photo*)

Many plants like fittonia, maranta, and ferns grow better in glass containers than in a room. And there are plants like selaginellas and sinningias that need high humidity and thrive in a covered garden—a pickle jar with a lid or a bottle with a stopper.

Selection of plants is vital in these miniature gardens. It takes many plants to make an attractive landscape. Choose plants that grow well together under the same conditions. Ferns, selaginellas, and fittonias need the high humidity of a covered garden. Cacti and succulents live for years in bottoms of glass percolators or candy jars without lids. Large goldfish bowls with rich soil are perfect homes for miniature geraniums, roses, or azaleas.

Leaky aquariums unfit for fish are ideal for plants. The tanks lend themselves beautifully to many kinds of landscapes—desert, woodland, and so on. To prepare an aquarium for planting, spread some small stones or tiny pieces of pots (shards) over the bottom. Put in some charcoal granules and cover them with a thin layer of peat moss. Then add about 3 inches of soil. Build the soil into gentle slopes or natural mounds. A flat terrain is dull. Dig some holes and insert plants; add some pebbles for paths. Use creeping varieties like baby-tears (*helxine soleiroli*) as a ground cover. Small rocks and a few figurines will complete the setting.

Bottle gardens require more planting preparation. Generally, the opening of the bottle is small, and patience and a steady

37. A glass bubble filled with popular house plants will thrive for many months. (*Roche photo*) 38. A dome garden with a thriving ivy plant. Lid is lifted occasionally to permit air into the garden. (*Author photo*)

hand are needed to create a striking picture. With these gardens, it is a good idea to have some knowledge of the rate of growth of the plants used. Sufficient space must be allowed for development. Use young plants; they are easy to manage and have a better chance than mature specimens to adjust to new conditions.

Start the garden by covering the base of the container with tiny stones mixed with charcoal granules. Put in a small amount of peat moss. Tip the bottle from side to side so the moss covers the stones. Then with a kitchen funnel add soil. Use dry soil so it will flow through the funnel into position without spattering the sides of the container.

To put the plants in place, a long thin tool is necessary. Chopsticks or heavy-gauge wire can be used, but it requires a very talented hand to use them and get the plants into the ground. There is a tool at hardware stores (used to pick up bolts and screws from car motors) that will help you do the job easily. It is called a pick-up tool—a long flexible wire with a retractable claw on one end and a plunger on the other end. Put the claw around the collar of the plants and press the plant into the soil. Allow the claw to retract while the tool is still in the bottle, and with the blunt edge pat the soil into place. Now, with a soft artist's paintbrush, brush excess dirt off plant foliage. Then funnel water slowly into the garden; the soil should be moist but never soggy.

After planting, set the garden in a semishaded place. In a few days move it into light or sun according to the plants' requirements. With bottle gardens, moisture does not escape and water is needed only occasionally—perhaps about once every three months. If too much moisture collects on the glass and the soil becomes soggy, mildew can occur in plants. Merely uncover the garden—remove the lid, take out the stopper—for an hour a day until the inside dries out somewhat.

Large bottles—water jugs and glass chemical containers—are generally placed upright. However, if there is a stand for them (found in salvage stores and used to hold boats in bottles) some of them can be put on their sides.

With bottles with small openings, removing faded flowers and decayed leaves is a tedious operation. Yet it must be done to prevent fungus diseases from attacking plants. Use the pick-up tool and proceed carefully, trying not to disturb the plantings.

After a few years a bottle garden may become overgrown even if you used small plants at the start. Replanting is necessary. Do not try to dump the contents out of the bottle; it does not work. Lift each plant out with the tool. What went in small may now be large. Remove the plant by gently drawing it up with the tool with the roots and foliage dangling down so the leaves will naturally bunch together and pass through the neck of the bottle. Repot the plants for window decoration. Let the soil in the bottle dry out completely; then turn the bottle upside down and remove the soil.

Plants for Open Containers (brandy snifters, bubble bowls, aquariums, apothecary jars)

Abutilon hybrids (flowering maple). Soft gray-green leaves and paper-thin bell-shaped flowers make these appealing plants. Young plants bloom readily; many varieties.

Achimenes (rainbow flowers). Large group of charming performers with tubular flowers and velvet-soft foliage. Select small varieties.

Adromischus. Miniature succulents ideal for open gardens. Try A. *clavifolius* with club-shaped silver-green leaves or A. *maculatus*; thick chocolate-brown foliage.

Aglaonema pictum. Outstanding foliage species with blue-green leaves splashed with silver.

Aloe brevifolia. A member of the lily family with sharp spiny leaves. Good accent plant.

Begonias. A large group with many fine miniatures. Try B. *boweri* with green leaves stitched with black, B. 'Chance' with mottled leaves and pink blooms. Also good are B. *dregei*, bronze-red foliage and nice branching habit and B. *rotundifolia* with apple-green leaves and pink flowers.

Crassula. A varied group of succulents with many miniatures. I recommend *C. cooperi* with tufts of pointed leaves and *C. schmidti*, a handsome pink-leaved species.

Cryptanthus. A group of bromeliads that are decorative and beautifully colored. Try these for real satisfaction: *C. bivittatus* with salmon-rose striped foliage, *C. bromelioides tricolor* with multicolored leaves, and *C. zonatus* with zebra bands of silver and green.

Cyanotis somaliensis. Bright green leaves edged with white fuzz. An oddity.

Dyckia fosteriana. A bromeliad with silver-spined leaves.

Euphorbia 'Bojeri.' (Dwarf crown of thorns). Dark green leaves and vivid red bracts. Dependable to bloom.

Faucaria tigrina. Lovely little succulent whose leaves resemble a tiger jaw.

Oxalis. Tropicals with buttercup-like flowers. *O. hedysaroides rubra* with butter-yellow flowers and *O. henrei (herrerae)* with tiny yellow flowers are good ones.

Rebutia minuscula. An amenable cactus that bears fiery red flowers.

Saintpaulia (African violet). A large popular family with many delightful miniatures that thrive in glass. Try these: 'Honeyette,' a fine red-lavender; 'Tinkle,' with lavender blooms; 'Tiny Bells,' a brilliant dark blue.

Plants for Closed Containers

Acorus gramineus pusillus. Tufts or iris-like leaves. Looks like grass in bottles.

Adiantum hispidulum. One of the many useful ferns with dark green branching fronds.

Allophyton mexicanum. Dark green oval leaves and bright lavender flowers.

Alternanthera versicolor. Pink, green, and white wrinkled foliage; nice color for garden.

Calathea argyraea. Low and compact with blotched green leaves laced with silver. Stunning.

Cissus striata (grape ivy). A lacy climber with scalloped leaves; tough to beat in a closed garden.

Erythroides nobilis argynoneurus. One of the charming jewel orchids with gray-green leaves etched with silver.

Fittonia verschaffeltii (mosaic plant). Velvety green leaves laced with veins of contrasting colors.

Hedera helix species. Ivy is always appealing in the closed garden, especially the wavy edged crinkly varieties. Many to choose from; see growers' catalogues.

Malpighia coccigera (miniature holly). Small glossy green leaves and whitish pink flowers.

Pellaea rotundifolia (button fern). Dark green round leaves on wiry stems. Highly recommended.

Peperomia. A large group with many miniatures.

Pilea. Many creepers in this family; branching stems and colored and patterned leaves. *P. nummulariaefolia, P. microphylla,* and *P. depressa* all good.

Pteris ensiformis 'Victoriae.' Showy silver and dark-green foliage.

Rosa. Miniature varieties increase in popularity daily. Many varieties.

Saxifraga sarmentosa (strawberry geranium). Rosettes of round silver-veined leaves.

Selaginella kraussiana brownii. A true creeper with grass-green foliage.

Sinningia pusilla. Miniature gloxinia; a gem with soft round leaves and pale lavender flowers. Many new varieties.

Tradescantia multiflora (inch-plant). Creeper with dark green foliage.

Gardens in Stone Trays

Miniature gardens in sinks or troughs make charming out-door pictures to decorate a landscape. Unfortunately, the availability of a suitable container deters many people from enjoying this hobby. Concrete sinks and troughs are difficult to find. But concrete birdbaths and stone containers are available, and if they are 4 to 6 inches deep, they can certainly be used. Even terra-cotta tapered bowls are a possibility and, of course, you can make your own concrete containers.

Whatever container you use, be sure it has plenty of holes

39. Here a stone sink garden is host to several flowering plants; a feature in this small walled area. (*Photo by Roy Elliot*)

in the bottom for drainage, that it is strong and weather resistant and deep enough to hold small trees and shrubs. A big advantage of a sink garden is that it is at waist level and stooping and squatting to tend it are not necessary. And, too, the garden is elevated and easy to see. Use bricks, concrete blocks, or pedestal posts to support the miniature landscape.

The sink garden is prepared by covering the bottom of the container with about ½-inch layer of tiny stones. Then add peat moss to cover them. Water the peat so it forms a blanket over the stones. Then add soil to about one-third the depth of the container. Press the soil in place to eliminate air pockets, and shape the landscape with hills and valleys or a level area if you prefer. Move the potted plants around in the garden until you find just the right places for them. Then take them from the pots and set them in permanently. Add small stones, paths, and other props needed to create the setting.

A stone garden is heavy filled with soil and plants. Plant it in its permanent place. Give the miniature landscape some sun for part of the day. A good spot for it is under a high branched tree.

While stone gardens are essentially for outdoors, some of them can be grown in an unheated, but not freezing, room where there is good light. In winter, most of them will need some protection from extreme cold or heavy rains. Cover them with plastic cloth or store them in a cold frame or use oak leaves or hay over them.

Watering depends on the weather, the types of plants in the tray, the soil mix, and the size of the garden. Large ones need less frequent attention than small ones.

There is a wealth of plant material for sink gardens. Alpines and rock plants are charming, native plants lovely, and small trees and shrubs are always desirable. Miniature annuals and perennials, tiny bulbs, and aquatic plants are other possibilities. All kinds of landscapes can be created in miniature—formal, desert, oriental, woodland—and so on.

Mail-order specialists in alpine and rockery plants list hundreds of varieties for tiny gardens. (See list at end of book.)

40. A flowering quince in a handsome bonsai, container
needs little care; it is decorative all year.
(*Photo by Bob Behme*)

Bonsai

The art of bonsai—growing dwarfed potted plants—is truly
beautiful and requires skill. When you grow small plants in
trays or dishes, the container is as important as the plant.
Generally, pottery containers in the earth colors—green, gray,
brown—are preferred. The inside of the dish should be un-

glazed, the outside can be glazed or unglazed. The color of the container should complement the color of the plant. For example, a red maple looks best in a brown or gray dish, a green pine in a brown container. An upright plant looks best in a round or square container, and spreading plants are handsome in shallow dishes. A heavy-trunked tree needs a pot with equal depth and width, and plants that are very gnarled—with growth on a vertical plane—are stunning in rectangular or oval pots.

There are shallow pots and deep ones in many shapes and sizes—rectangular, square, round, oval, hexagonal—for bonsai growing. And while there are authentic decorative bonsai con-

41. This wooden container is perfect for these small trees. (*Photo by Bob Behme*)

tainers, these are generally expensive and not easy to find. Whatever container you use, remember that there must always be a pleasing balance between the size and shape of the plant and the container it grows in.

Traditional Japanese bonsai plants—native hardy shrubs and trees whose foliage changes with the seasons—are expensive and difficult to obtain. However, there are many inexpensive plants that adapt to the bonsai type of growth. Miniature woody begonias, tiny ficus species, or, as a matter of fact, any interestingly shaped plant with sculptural growth can be used.

For bonsai, look for species with interesting trunks or stems and well-placed lower branches. Select small-leaved varieties that are in keeping with miniature landscapes. Form and scale are vitally important in the potted plant and in the composition formed by the plant and the container. This is a work of art in miniature; every leaf and twig is under scrutiny.

Other quick bonsai subjects are nursery container juniper or Norway spruce or mugo pine. Plants have to be pruned drastically, and the gardener must have a good eye as to what to cut away and what to leave growing. And this is a matter of experience.

Ordinary potting soil can be used for bonsai plants—the kind you get in packages—but I find a soil on the "poor" side with some clay and sand to be better for most dwarf plants.

Root pruning is done initially to keep plants healthy in small dishes; the idea is to maintain the plant in a small size, so do not feed them. Training branches in place with wire, and pruning plants to desired shapes that are pleasing and handsome are necessary maintenance with bonsai growing.

While pruning and shaping plants is important, good environmental conditions are necessary too. Most species need an airy but not a windy place. Some shade is necessary during the heat of the day, and the soil during the growing season must be kept evenly moist. Even in winter, soil should be damp to the touch. In extreme winters, some protection will be needed for the bonsai garden. A deep cold frame or an unheated, but not freezing, room is necessary.

42. A round bonsai dish sets off this attractive maple. (*Photo by Bob Behme*)

It is difficult to suggest plants for bonsai; there are so many for bonsai growing. However, there are some that will adapt better than others. For example, some of the Kurume azaleas have lovely sculptural growth and can be pruned drastically without harm to them. They are a wealth of color in bloom. Flowering quince is always a spectacle in spring, and small spruce, juniper, pine, and hemlock have endearing qualities when properly pruned and potted in a suitable container. Even miniature begonias can make striking bonsai pictures; so can *malpighia coccigera* and *carissa grandiflora* with lush green leaves. Do not be afraid to try the unusual; if you find the plant is not suitable, it can be repotted for window growing.

Herb Gardens

Most people know that herbs are useful for cooking. But few people realize that many herbs are also attractive plants. Tarragon, with dark green leaves on spreading branches, is most attractive; thyme, bushy and full, is charming in a hanging basket.

Herbs need a somewhat sunny place at the window with a temperature of 50° to 76° F. and average humidity, say, 40 per cent. Use a well-drained mealy soil of equal parts garden loam, sand, and leaf mold. Packaged soil mixes are also satisfactory.

You can buy herbs already started in thumbnail pots at nurseries or you can sow seed. If you start your own herbs, provide 60 to 70 per cent humidity and an average temperature of 76° F. day and night. Herbs can be grown in any container—standard clay pot, planter box—but it is more interesting to have them in unusual containers: a clay cassolette or a wire basket used for draining vegetables. Or group small pots of herbs together in a large clay saucer. Keep the foliage washed clean with tepid water, turn the plants at the windows about once a week, and let some fresh air into the growing area. Herbs like chives, parsley, mint, and such can be snipped from and used from the pot, leafy herbs are ready to be dried when flower buds begin to form. Merely dry them until crumbly and then store them in Mason or other airtight jars. Label and put in a shaded place.

HERBS

Chives
Sweet basil
Chervil
Dill
Fennel
Mint
Oregano
Parsley
Rosemary
Summer savory
Sage
Tarragon
Thyme

 *7. Plants for Decoration*

Living plants in handsome containers are superb accents for any room. They make a bare window sing with color, decorate a garden room, and transform an enclosed atrium or court into a pleasant greenery. Even one large potted plant strategically placed is striking.

Old favorites like Boston fern and philodendron are still available, and new plants are taking their place indoors too. Specimen palms and cycads, bamboo and small trees in glamorous containers are necessary interior furnishings.

New concepts in architecture have created new uses for plants. Large glass windows and expanses of unadorned walls demand living plants. The organic school of building—natural wood and stone—is lovely but somewhat hard and sharp; we have to soften line and detailing with plants. A small-leaved ficus is lacy and delicate and adds the necessary charm to make a room inviting. A large bromeliad with multicolored foliage against a white wall is dramatic, and the grace and beauty of a palm cannot be denied in any situation.

The container should blend with the room setting. There

43. This room features plants in white plastic pots. (*Window Shade Mfg. Assn.*)

are pots with outside design motifs—oriental, Mediterranean, contemporary—so choose one that fits the setting.

Interior designers depend upon large green plants in containers to decorate offices, stores, and lobbies. Where pedestrian traffic needs direction, where room areas need separation, container plants do the job. First impressions are important in places of business, and live plants give the customer a welcome feeling.

At Windows

The window garden by its very nature is generally a small, intimate area, a colorful spot in a room. Shelves, brackets, hanging baskets, and suspension poles with trays are places for plants. Avoid cumbersome tubs that take up space. This is a place for many plants in simple containers to bring lots of color to the window. While clay pots can be used for plants, white or pastel-colored plastic containers are fine too. But do not select clear plastic; light coming through the window will show soil and root networks which are hardly attractive. I have seen rows of opaque white plastic pots of the same size and color at windows that made a pleasing arrangement.

For a different effect, use bamboo or rattan pot covers; wood lends warmth to a setting. Strawberry jars or other novelty containers simply do not look good at windows, nor do large wooden tubs. Keep plants to 6- or 8-inch pots, in scale with the average window. If you have an exceptionally large glass expanse, then of course large pots can be used.

Whether you select clay or plastic pots, buy the appropriate saucer for them to protect window sills. While the unglazed saucer is not completely moistureproof, it still protects surfaces against stains. The saucer painted black helps to prevent stains on wood surfaces.

Keep all containers spotless. Scrub clay pots with Brillo pads and hot water to remove stains and algae. Plastic pots can be wiped clean with a detergent.

Look for the new fern pots at nurseries. They are handsome and are small at the bottom and larger at the top. They take up less space at the window than a conventional container and still have adequate space for soil (see Chapter 1).

Here are some dependable plants for the window garden:

Window Plants

Aechmea fasciata. The popular Silver King with mottled silver and gray foliage and a pink flower crown.

Ascocentrum miniatum (rainbow orchid). A dwarf orchid with bright orange springtime flowers.

Begonias. Large group with many small and medium plants. For flowers, select the angelwings with showy cascades of pink or red, orange or white bloom. The semperflorens (wax begonias) are desirable, too, with colorful foliage and abundant bloom. For foliage, rhizomatous and hairy-leaved varieties brighten any window and these plants adjust to adverse conditions.

Cacti. Carefree plants that stay small for years. Many species useful in the window garden including: echinocereus, mammillaria, and notocactus.

Caladiums. A large group of multicolored foliage plants. Leaves are arrow-shaped, papery. Try 'Ace of Spades,' red, white, and rose, 'Debutante' with white-and-green foliage, or 'Fire chief,' a pink-leaved variety.

Caryota (fish-tail palm). A handsome palm with edge-shaped fronds. Graceful, and always lovely in a white tub.

Chamaedorea elegans bella (bamboo palm). A popular palm, with graceful, arching fronds.

Cocus weddelliana (coco palm). Dwarf, with feathery yellow-green foliage. A good palm.

Dendrobium pierardii. A deciduous, easy-to-grow, trailing orchid with large lavender flowers in March or April. Needs coolness (45° F.) in late fall to encourage budding. Grow in fir bark.

Dieffenbachia. Amenable house plants. *D. exotica* has mottled green and white foliage. *D. bowmannii*, chartreuse leaves, and *D. splendens*, velvety green foliage with white spots.

Dracaena. Many suitable window species, the following outstanding: *D. deremensis Warneckii* with gray and green leaves; *D. fragrans massangeana* (corn plant) has cream-colored stripes on broad leaves; and *D. godseffiana* bears green and yellow foliage.

Ferns. Graceful, always desirable plants. Highly recommended are *adiantum cuneatum*, old favorite with dark green fronds; *A. tenerum* 'Wrightii,' a stellar maidenhair fern; and *asplenium nidus* (bird's-nest fern) with spatular-shaped evergreen fronds. Also desirable are: *nephrolepis exaltata*, sword fern with long pendent fronds, and *woodwardia orientalis*, the chain fern.

44. A simple bronze pot holds a dracaena; note the handsome rattan and rawhide tripod holder. (*McGuire Furniture Co.*)

Ficus. Two outstanding species here: *F. elastica decora*, with oval glossy green leaves, and *F. lyrata* (fiddle-leaf fig) with leathery dark green foliage.

Oncidium ampliatum (turtle orchid). A medium-sized orchid with wands of small bright-yellow flowers in early spring. Grows easily; pot in fir bark.

Oncidium splendidum. With thick, succulent leaves and handsome brown and yellow flowers, this amenable orchid is always desirable at the window. Grow in small pots in fir bark.

Philodendron. Popular foliage plants for indoors. *P. Andreanum* has arrow-shaped leaves; *P. cordatum,* heart-shaped glossy green leaves; and *P. wendlandii,* dense rosettes of waxy green leaves. Many other varieties available.

Tillandsia juncea. Graceful rosette growth and bizarre purple blooms.

Vriesia splendens (flaming sword). An amenable bromeliad, with apple-green foliage and orange flower head.

Garden Rooms and Atriums

The garden room or solarium is now the extra room in the home. Surrounded by greenery, it is a retreat from the busy world. This area depends on potted plants to give it its character. Interior landscaping with plants lifts a room from the ordinary to the extraordinary.

The garden room will be the place where guests will gather for cocktails, where you will have morning coffee. And what is more cheerful than bright flowers to welcome a gray day? Choose containers and plants that are large and showy. Keep them beautifully groomed. They are always on display. Search for a large jardiniere, an unusual urn for a corner. Then, perhaps, some smaller pots of the same size and shape, on a bed of white gravel, in a planter bin along a wall. Use one of the fine standards—geranium, fuchsia, rose—in a large white tub on the opposite wall to balance a setting. And a pair of small espaliers in concrete urns is always charming at the entrance to the room.

Let your imagination go and have all kinds of plants and pots in the garden room. And by all means do not forget hanging baskets of ferns and flowering plants for eye-level interest.

A garden room is exactly that—a garden and a room. Containers make it possible to have this garden indoors. Manufacturers of containers have responded to the challenge with a brand-new array of tubs and pots, jardinieres, and urns for these areas. Don't miss the opportunity to have this extra living space.

45. A garden room with specimen indoor plants is charming and warm.
(*Roedel photo, House Beautiful*)

Plants for Garden Rooms

Aechmea ramosa. Variegated leaves and gaudy flower bracts make this an outstanding container plant.

Aerides crispum. A good medium-sized orchid with strap leaves and lavender flowers in spring. Grow in fir bark.

Agave attenuata. A handsome succulent with sword-shaped green leaves that will thrive for years in a tub.

Alocasia. Large leaved foliage plants well known for their tropical appearance. Somewhat touchy, but beautiful.

Blechnum brasiliense. Big fern to fill a corner with fresh green. Easy to grow.

Cycas revoluta. Dark, shiny, green leaves; nice manner of growth.

Dracaena marginata. Splendid decorator plant with branching growth and sword-shaped rosettes of dark green leaves edged in red.

Epiphyllum (orchid cactus). Outstanding and well known for their mammoth flowers, epiphyllums bloom in May or June, come in a rainbow of colors. Try 'Polar Bear,' 'Flower Song' or 'Cup of Gold.' 'Bacchus' and 'Harmony' are good too.

Ficus benjamina. A fine small tree with small leaves and gnarled growth. Loses leaves annually but will recover.

Gesneriads. A whole group of lovely flowering plants including rechstieneria, gloxinia, kohleria, smithianthina. All need warmth and some sun to prosper.

Guzmania lingulata. Bright colorful bracts for six months. Rosette growth.

Hedychium coronarium (butterfly lily). Pure white flowers and leafy canes to 6 feet. Needs sun, heavy watering.

Heliconia angustifolia. A member of the banana family with leathery leaves and orange-red bracts. Stunning in bloom in summer.

Heliconia aurantiaca. About 3 feet tall with leathery leaves and erect orange bracts tipped green. Only recently available.

Howea forsteriana. This palm has pendent flat leaves from a central stem. Grows quickly.

Lycaste aromatica. One of the smaller orchids, with paper thin foliage and bright yellow fragrant flowers.

Oncidium splendidum. Unusual orchids with succulent dark green leaves and wands of bright yellow flowers. Impossible to kill. Grow in fir bark.

Phaius grandifolius (nun's orchid). Decorative foliage and large multicolored flowers.

Philodendron monstera deliciosa (Swiss-cheese plant). The most popular philodendron, with mammoth scalloped leaves— a well-known specimen that is always handsome. Trim occasionally, so plant does not get leggy.

Rhapis excelsa. Indestructible, with green, fan-shaped leaves. A popular palm.

Plants to Decorate Rooms

Lush green leaves, attractive textures, and pleasing patterns are what makes foliage plants so desirable in the home. These are stellar house plants because they grow in subdued light with minimum care. Some plants like agaves and bromeliads have a sculptural look, while others, like ferns and palms, are graceful and airy. Each plant needs its own kind of container; for example, the skeletal quality of dizygotheca requires a plain but somewhat formal tub. The spiraling and graceful palm needs a tight-lipped container, the feathery bamboo is at its best in a wooden box, while the delicate scallop-leaved Japanese maple is handsome in a tub.

The tub or box for the plant is an integral part of the room furnishings. Often a unique container is a considerable investment. Since it can cost as much as a piece of furniture, choose it with taste. Properly selected, it will be a beautiful addition to a room for many years.

Here are some fine room plants selected from hundreds of species because they have some outstanding feature or withstand adverse conditions.

46. Elegant rattan planters with graceful dizygotheca are charming and attractive at this room entrance. (*McGuire Furniture Co.*)

Agave Americana marginata. Variegated-type century plant. Broad lance-shaped leaves; a bold accent. Easy to grow; can remain in same pot for years. Give it a round clay container. Overlooked, but a dramatic plant.

Araucaria excelsa (Norfolk pine). Can grow to 7 feet, with lovely needle growth. Looks like a Christmas tree, and is highly ornamental in a white tub.

Chamaedorea erumpens (bamboo palm). A large palm that looks like a fern. Has willowy dark green fronds and grows readily indoors. Looks good in any pot.

Clivia miniata (Kafir lily). A low-growing broad-leaved green plant that greets spring with brilliant orange flowers. *Does bloom indoors* and likes to be pot bound.

Dizygotheca elegantissima (spider aralia). A difficult-to-grow but exquisite plant, with lacy fronds of delicately scalloped leaves. Can grow very tall. Keep out of sun but in a bright light, and never let soil get dry or soggy. Needs a clay pot.

Dracaena marginata (decorator plant). Well known and frightfully expensive. Branching plant with sculptural quality. Shiny lance-shaped leaves edged red. Slow growing, durable, and one of the best.

Ficus benjamina (banyan tree). To 7 feet with small leaves and a branching habit. Lacy and delicate. Loses leaves indoors in winter. Keep barely moist until new growth starts. Needs a large tub.

Ficus lyrata (fiddle-leaf fig). A fine tough plant with fiddle-shaped leathery leaves on a central trunk. Keep on the dry side.

Ficus retusa (laurel fig). An attractive pot plant with rubbery elliptical leaves. Does well indoors.

Howea fosteriana (paradise palm). A popular pot plant with graceful fronds on slender stalks. Slow growing and does well indoors.

Pandanus Veitchii (cork-screw pine). A spiral arrangement of long prickly sword-shaped glossy green leaves. Takes adverse conditions and thrives in same pot for many years. A well-grown plant makes a handsome accent. Don't overlook this one.

Philodendron bipinnatifidum (finger-leaf philodendron). One of the nicest in the group, with ornamental leaves that are deeply scalloped. Let soil dry out between waterings. Will thrive without sun.

Philodendron monstera deliciosa (Swiss-cheese plant). A robust grower with handsome leaves, leathery, thick, and glossy green. Plant has tendency to get leggy. Use a mild fertilizer during growth.

47. A sweet potato vine in an unusual pedestal container. (*Roche photo*)

Yucca aloifolia (Spanish bayonet). Don't let the name scare you. Leaves margined ivory with a tinge of red. Look for mature specimen. Seldom seen indoors, but certainly a unique accent.

Lobbies, Offices, and Stores

Recently, container maufacturers have offered many large boxes and tubs in several different materials for institutional use. Here the container is chosen first and the plant is then fitted to the pot.

Most buildings are somewhat severe in architecture with glass and concrete walls. To soften the geometric lines, living plants now beautify many lobbies, stores, and offices. Planters are used to direct traffic, or where room areas need separation, or when a focal point is needed. Tubs and boxes are often seen and new designs in many sizes and shapes—square, rectangular, hexagonal—in colors, are being introduced.

In addition to old favorites like palms and ferns, new species are constantly introduced, and it is not unusual to see camellia or rhododendron trees brightening an area. Seasonal displays of flowering plants are seen too. It all adds up to an entirely new field of decorating with plants. Shopping centers, and condominiums have gardens, and even libraries, schools, and other public buildings are being filled with plants.

The selection of plants is vital for public areas. The ones chosen must, in most cases, be able to withstand adverse conditions—dust, soot, smoke, and drafts from doors opening or closing. Further, unless artificial lighting has been strategically placed to help plants grow, they must live without bright light. Some plants are able to survive for many months in such an environment; others will not.

If plants have the help of incandescent or fluorescent light, most of them respond and live for many months where otherwise they would perish in a few weeks. New lighting that does not radiate too much heat is now available and can safely be used for plants at a distance of 2 to 3 feet.

Certain palms and ferns do exceptionally well in public buildings, and so do some of the dracaena species. Bromeliads are known as institutional plants because they tolerate untoward conditions and still stay beautiful. Surprisingly, many of the large succulents—agaves, aloes—and some of the cacti do well too.

Philodendrons, long-time favorite house plants, as a rule do not do well in buildings and eventually they have to be replaced. The misconception about their hardiness started because they can tolerate something less than sunshine, but basically they are temperamental about drafts, watering, and temperature changes. Dieffenbachias are another ill choice; they are somewhat difficult in the home where we can watch them and are highly susceptible to wilting from sudden drafts—a common happening in public buildings. On the other hand, podocarpus species do exceptionally well with minimum care.

The subject of living plants in architect-designed planters for modern interiors has only recently been recognized. New information and research is being released periodically.

48. The sleek lines of this aluminum planter make it a perfect container for offices, public buildings and lobbies as well as for the modern home. (*Leyse Aluminum Company*)

(*California Association of Nurserymen*)

Special Section: Some Excellent Container Plants

Although all kinds of plants can be grown in containers, some do better and are easier to grow than others. Geraniums and fuchsias are all-around plants equally good for indoors and outdoors in tubs, boxes, and hanging baskets. Tuberous begonias surpass most summer flowering plants outdoors, and succulents are natural container plants.

Geraniums

The appeal of geraniums cannot be denied. They are grown everywhere and anywhere. And it seems that in all locations, regardless of climate, they flourish. In vibrant colors of scarlet, red, or pastel shades of pink and rose, there are few plants that can match geraniums for color and ease of culture. They are excellent outdoors and can make a really striking display in the proper container. Indoors, too, they are charming.

There are all kinds of geraniums—zonals with circular markings on rounded leaves, scented-leaved kinds, ivy-leaved and

131

Lady Washington types. There are unusual ones, cactus type, climbers, and the new carefree kinds. The selection is limitless, and practically all of them are well suited to container gardening.

ZONAL GERANIUMS

These are the geraniums most often seen. In window-boxes or in the garden as pot plants they have been with us all our lives. There are many fascinating flower forms in single and double types.

The single and double zonals (so named for the unusual dark zonal markings on the leaves) offer a wide range of color. They are perfect plants where a single color scheme is needed, grow equally well in pot, or tub, or box, and even look good in clay pots in ring holders at eye level on fences. Here is a sampling:

White

'Summer Cloud'
'White Magic'
'Starlight'

Coral and Salmon

'Festival'
'Inspiration'
'Shimmer'
'Springtime'
'Flair'
'Honeymoon'
'Lady of Spain'

Scarlet

'Aztec'
'Fireglow'
'Toyon'
'Flame'

Orange

'Halloween'
'Harvest Moon'
'Token'

Rose Pink and Carmine

'Genie'
'Pink Giant'
'Shocking'
'Luster'

132

VARIEGATED GERANIUMS

Variegated geraniums set among foliage plants offer contrast and pattern to a window-box grouping. There are many different kinds of leaf coloring—green and yellow, yellow and brown, silver-leaved. What you use depends on the container, where you want the plants, and what kind of effect you want. Certainly the variegated geraniums are showy. Some of the prettiest:

'Bronze Beauty No. 2.' Yellow and green and bronze.
'Crystal Palace Gem.' Yellow and bright green.
'Jubilee.' Yellow-green and red-brown.
'Skies of Italy.' Golden tricolor.
'Mrs. Cox.' Vermilion and purple.

An indoor garden of scented-leaved geraniums is a small treasure. The scent of the crushed leaves is wonderful, and there is nothing more decorative than a group of these geraniums in a small tub at the window or in a unique container on the coffee table.

Plants grow quickly, and some need plenty of vertical room. Popular kinds include the nutmeg with white flowers and round leaves, peppermint type with large velvety leaves, and the rose- and lemon-scented varieties.

For outdoor decoration, scented potted geraniums have many uses. They can accent an entrance or path, or can be trained to make handsome standards.

IVY-LEAVED AND LADY WASHINGTON TYPES

Baskets of ivy-leaved geraniums stop traffic at flower shows. As hanging plants they are unsurpassed. Grown under favorable conditions, they flower profusely for many months. In colors of pink, lavender, cerise, purple, and white, the ivy-leaved geraniums trailing from a window-box are a cascade of color.

These geraniums thrive in California where warm days and cool nights keep them lush and healthy. My plants grow in partial shade in average humidity. They are versatile, and I grow them in hanging baskets, in flower boxes on the deck, and in the house too.

Lady Washingtons, although not as easy to grow as most geraniums, are frequently seen as patio and terrace decorations in California and the Northwest. These are splendid plants with colorful flowers—white tinged with pink, sparkling reds, and pastel pinks. They prefer cool nights and warm bright days and need shelter from wind and noon sun. New cultivars appear frequently, one more beautiful than the last.

CULTURE

These are general rules for geraniums, the way I grow them in California. Specific culture varies, depending upon the conditions and what kind of geraniums you grow.

I use a good garden loam consisting of 3 parts humus, 1 part leafmold, and a 5-inch pot of bone meal for each bushel of mix. I fertilize my tubbed plants with a 5-10-5 fertilizer applied every other watering. Sunshine is best for the plants, although many bloom only in bright light. However, protection against torrid noonday sun is essential.

My geraniums are flooded with water and then allowed to dry out completely before I water them again. They are always potted in containers that have a generous amount of drainage material. If soil becomes waterlogged, the leaves turn yellow.

Tuberous *Begonias*

Begonias with tuberous roots have gained world-wide recognition, and rightly so. In full bloom, they are a sight to behold, a veritable sea of color. They bloom profusely in all colors except blue, and at the height of the season are a spectacle. Whether used singly or in pots grouped together, they are splendid decoration in boxes and tubs, in hanging baskets—in almost any container—for patio, terrace, atrium, and garden.

There are a number of flower forms:

Camelliaflora, most often seen as a flat flower with incredibly large blooms in all typical colors. There are endless varieties. These are magnificent in window-boxes, a solid row of glowing color.

Cristata flowers are big, single, with a tufted crest on each petal, often a different color from the petal itself. Handsome in standard clay pots, use three or four on a terrace floor or in a corner.

Fimbriata has frayed petals resembling carnations. Though the flowers are smaller than the camellia form, the plants are more robust. Architectural pots and low white bowls show them off to great advantage.

Marginata flowers have two forms: crispa marginata, frilled singles with the same color edges, and double marginata with petals lined and edged with bands of contrasting colors. Lovely for redwood boxes.

Picotee with smaller flowers has petals lined with another color bleeding into the predominant color.

Rose form has a high center of petals inside, and outer petals flared back like a rose. Dramatic, best in plain containers.

Named varieties include:

'Black Knight,' spectacular crimson flowers.

'Chinook,' a beautiful double ruffled form.

'Flambeau,' lovely double orange blooms.

'Mandarin,' double salmon flowers.

'Rosado,' deeply frilled and ruffled pink blooms.

'Royal Flush,' a brilliant scarlet form.

MULTIFLORAS AND PENDULAS

The multifloras are a smaller group, compact in growth with many flowers, either single or semidouble. They are excellent for garden borders. Easy to grow, they do not need as much humidity as tuberous kinds, and they tolerate more heat and sun.

Pendulas are trailing tuberous begonias, usually listed in catalogues as hanging basket or Lloydi types. They bloom a long time, sometimes into fall, and need warmth, humidity, and protection from wind and sun. Pinch out young growth early in the season to promote trailing growth.

Like geraniums and fuchsias, trailing begonias are superlative basket plants. It is hard to find more handsome flowers for outdoor decoration.

HOW TO GROW AND PROPAGATE TUBEROUS BEGONIAS

In March select large or middle-sized tubers—those an inch or more in diameter. Put a 2-inch layer of peat moss and sand (1-to-2 ratio) in a wooden flat or other suitable box. Set the tubers 2 inches apart and about ½ inch deep, with dented side up, in the medium. Cover them with about ¼ inch of the mix. Roots develop from bottom, sides, and top so be sure that the tuber is covered. Place the flat in good light in 60 to 70° F. and keep the rooting medium barely wet. Too much water causes the tubers to rot. When the sprouts are about 2 inches tall (in about two weeks), shift them to shallow pots. (I use 4-inch azalea pots with a layer of stone and loose soil). Then move the potted begonias to a cooler place. Water them sparingly.

In a few weeks, around the middle of May, the begonias will be ready for larger, but shallow, pots. Or if you plant them in boxes, use an 8-inch depth. My tuberous begonias do best in standard clay pots, in wall brackets, on fences, or in redwood hanging baskets where air circulates around the container. Like many of the orchids from high altitudes, tuberous begonias need good air circulation.

Give the plants some scattered sunshine. They survive heat during the day but must have cool nights, 55 to 60° F. If summer days are very hot, mist the area around the plants (not the leaves). Water begonias heavily on bright days, not so much in cloudy weather. When they are growing well, start using a fertilizer mixed half strength every second week.

After blooming, when leaves turn dry and yellow, water sparingly but let growth continue for as long as possible. Then take

136

the tubers from the containers and wash and dry them thoroughly. Store them in shallow boxes—I put them in metal baking dishes—at 45 to 50° F. Give them good air circulation but keep them in shade. Keep them dry until the following spring.

There are two ways to propagate tuberous begonias: by dividing tubers or from stem cuttings.

When bulbs start to mature in spring and show sprouts, cut tubers into as many pieces as there are eyes. Do this as soon as new shoots are clearly seen but not yet growing. Dust sections with powdered charcoal and let them dry for a few days. Then pot them 1 inch deep in sand and put them in a semishady warm place.

For stem cuttings, with a sharp knife take 3- to 4-inch cuttings of new growth. Dust the cut surfaces with powdered charcoal before potting. Cuttings taken in spring and summer root in about a month in sand and peat moss in a bright warm spot. When roots have developed, pot the cuttings similar to tuber division.

Fuchsias

Whether in individual pots, window-boxes, or in hanging baskets, fuchsias always put on a show. There are hundreds of varieties in rose, purple, and white shades in either upright or hanging types. The flowers have a certain splendor unlike any other blossom. And most important, fuchsias do grow and bloom in shade.

The hanging basket kinds offer dramatic color for little cost. Sometimes fuchsias are so floriferous, the flowers completely hide the container. There are hundreds of varieties and I would not dare select a few favorites. They are all good.

For specimen plants the upright growers are indeed handsome. In redwood boxes or stone tubs they sing out with color. Against a fence or terrace wall they make an excellent vertical accent. Many good varieties are to be found at nurseries.

Fuchsias trained to tree form match the beauty of the rose,

137

the splendor of azaleas. Start your own plant kept tied to a stake and at the desired height of 3 to 4 feet, pinch back the single stalk and allow it to grow. Or if this is too much work, buy plants already started. Fuchsias can also be trained into lovely espalier subjects.

CULTURE

Fuchsias are great favorites because they do bloom in shade; a north exposure suits them fine. Although they thrive under cool, moist conditions there are some that tolerate some heat.

Keep fuchsias wet at all times. On hot days I water them in the morning and again in the late afternoon. Because they require so much water, drainage must be perfect. Provide sufficient pot pieces or stones in the bottom of the container so excess water can drain from the soil. Use an acid soil and fertilize the plants every other week.

Succulents

Succulent plants are ideal for small wooden boxes, shallow bowls, or metal dishes. An indoor garden of succulents is easy to care for, always interesting. Remember these are drought-resistant plants that can go for days without water if we forget to tend to them. Outdoors in containers, succulents can be used for effective decoration of many kinds. There are tall ones, medium-sized plants, and small growers to fit every need, and because the color and texture of the foliage is so varied, unique planting can be achieved.

Redwood boxes, 2 to 4 inches deep and about 18 inches square are ideal for an arrangement of succulents. A 10- to 12-inch-diameter shallow clay pot is another good choice for them. Or for a different effect try a box full of the same plants rather than an assortment of plants. However, very large containers should be avoided; succulents do best in small ones. Round plants require round pots, while the tall-growing succulents need a pot half as wide as their height.

CULTURE

Soil for succulents should be lean and sandy. I use 2 parts coarse sand, 1 part loam, and 1 part leaf mold. This mix seems satisfactory for most of the plants I grow. Drainage in pots must be perfect for succulents, so I always work slowly and patiently when I pot them. I put drainage pieces in the bottom of the container; I also add a thin layer of crushed stone and some very small bits of charcoal.

The succulents do not need or, as a matter of fact, tolerate wet soil. It is best to grow them dry, perhaps watering them only once a week. There are a few kinds that do want excessive moisture, but the majority prefer a dry soil. Winter sunlight is good for the plants, direct summer rays should be avoided. The best location seems an east or west exposure. A great many succulents can be grown outside where temperatures do not go below 40° F. And there are others that tolerate 25° F. or lower. In winter rest them somewhat.

The succulent world is gigantic; there are over twenty-five families, thousands of plants. The ones I have are personal choices—I like the shape or color of the plants. It is impossible to list all good succulent plants. In Chapter 4 I have named some that are my favorites.

Here we have mentioned some of the better container plants; by no means have we talked about all of them. And if I have missed some of your favorites it is merely a matter of space, not choice. And, too, some plants that have not responded well for me may be a glowing success under your conditions. As mentioned earlier, almost any kind of plant can be grown in a container, so do experiment. It is part of the excitement of portable gardening.

Where to Buy Plants

Alberts & Merkel Bros., Inc.
P. O. Box 537
Boynton Beach, Fla. 33435

Orchids, bromeliads, and other tropical plants. Catalogue 50¢.

Buell's Greenhouses
Eastford, Conn. 06242

Gloxinias, African violets.

Burgess Seed & Plant Co., Inc.
67 E. Battle Creek St.
Galesburg, Mich. 49053

Many kinds of plants.

W. Atlee Burpee Co.
Philadelphia, Pa. 19132

Seeds and bulbs.

P. De Jager & Sons, Inc.
188 Asbury St.
S. Hamilton, Mass. 01982

Outstanding selection of bulbs.

Fantastic Gardens
9550 S.W. 67th Ave.
South Miami, Fla. 33030

Tropical plants, bromeliads.

Fennell Orchid Co.
26715 S.W. 157th Ave.
Homestead, Fla. 33030

Wide selection of orchids. Catalogue 50¢.

Where to Buy Plants

Fischer Greenhouses Linwood, N.J. 08221	African violets and other gesneriads.
Hauserman's Orchids Box 363 Elmhurst, Ill. 60218	Wide selection of species orchids.
Margaret Ilgenfritz Box 665 Monroe, Mich. 48161	Large selection of species orchids. Catalogue $1.00.
Kartuz Greenhouses 92 Chestnut St. Wilmington, Mass. 01887	House plants, especially bromeliads.
Logee's Greenhouses 55 North St. Danielson, Conn. 06239	All kinds of house plants. Catalogue 50¢.
Lyndon Lyon 14 Mutchler St. Dolgeville, N.Y. 13329	African violets, columneas.
Rod McLellan Co. 1450 El Camino Real S. San Francisco, Calif. 94080	Orchids.
Merry Gardens Camden, Maine 04843	Complete selection of house plants. Catalogue $1.00.
Oakhurst Gardens P. O. Box 444 Arcadia, Calif. 91008	Unusual bulbs, plants. Catalogue 50¢.
George W. Park Seed Co., Inc. Box 31 Greenwood, S.C. 29646	All kinds of house plants, seeds.
Julius Roehrs Co. East Rutherford, N.J. 07073	All kinds of plants.
Tinari Greenhouses 2325 Valley Road Bethayres, Pa. 19006	African violets and other plants.

Tropical Paradise Greenhouses
8825 W. 79th St.
Overland Park, Kans. 66200

Wide selection of house plants.

Wilson Bros.
Roachdale, Ind. 46172

Geraniums and other house plants.

Source List for Containers and Materials

Containers for plants are found at nursery and garden centers, patio shops, and specialty shops. They are also carried in the outdoor-living sections of many department stores. Mail-order houses and plant suppliers also furnish decorative and self-watering containers. And there are individual ceramists and potters who make individual pots.

Construction materials to build planters are at lumberyards, hardware stores, and local building-supply companies.

Decorative containers are available through several outlets; for information where they can be purchased, write to:

ARCHITECTURAL
POTTERY CO.
2020 S. Robertson Blvd.
Los Angeles, Calif. 90034

Architectural pots of many different sizes and shapes for indoors and outdoors.

PLANTAMATION INC.
136 E. 57th St.
New York, N.Y. 10022

Plantender containers, self-watering pots.

Kennebunk House
43 Fletcher St.
Dept. OG
Kennebunk, Maine 04043

Florabien water containers.

144

JoJan
Dept. F
4267 Via Marina
Marina Del Rey, Calif. 90291

Florabien water containers.

LEYSE ALUMINUM
COMPANY
203 Ellis Street
Kewaunee, Wisconsin

Aluminum planters.

SHEP
815 Main St.
Huntington Beach, Calif. 92646

Earthenware pots; many sizes and shapes.

CORNING GLASS WORKS
Corning, N.Y. 14830

Glass containers for large plants.

PLACET PRODUCTS
5000 W. 35th St.
Minneapolis, Minn. 55416

Decorative planters; many shapes and sizes.

CONCORD
WOODWORKING CO.
West Concord, Mass. 01781

Redwood planters.

A. L. RANDALL CO.
1325 W. Randolph St.
Chicago, Ill. 60607

Glass containers for terrariums.

 *Books to Read*

All About Miniature Plants and Gardens, Bernice Brilmayer, Double-
day, 1963.
Begonias, Indoors and Out, Jack Kramer, E. P. Dutton, 1967.
Bonsai, B. Behme, William Morrow, 1969.
Bonsai: Indoors and Out, Jerald P. Stowell, D. Van Nostrand, 1966.
Book of Cacti and Other Succulents, Claude Chidamian, Doubleday,
1958.
Bromeliads, the Colorful House Plants, Jack Kramer, D. Van Nos-
trand, 1965.
City Gardener, Philip Treux, Alfred A. Knopf, 1964.
Designing a Garden Today, J. E. Grant White, Abelard-Schuman,
1966.
Easy Gardening with Drought-resistant Plants, Arno and Irene Nehr-
ling, Hearthside, 1968.
Gardens Under Glass, J. Kramer, Simon & Schuster, 1969.
Joy of Geraniums, H. V. Wilson, Barrous, 1965.
Miniature Plants for Home and Greenhouse, Elvin McDonald, D. Van
Nostrand, 1963.
1000 Beautiful House Plants, J. Kramer, William Morrow, 1969.
Outdoor Gardening in Pots and Boxes, George Taloumis, D. Van Nos-
trand, 1962.

Shrubs and Trees for the Home Landscape, James Bush-Brown, Chilton, 1963.

Shrubs and Vines for American Gardens, Donald Wyman, Macmillan, 1970.

Small City Gardens, Brett, W. S., and Grant, H. K., Abelard-Schuman, 1968.

Succulents and Cactus, Lane Publishing, 1970.

Terrace and Courtyard Gardens, A. D. B. Wood, Collingridge, 1965.

Index

Index

Index

Index